625.   Klamkin, Charles
10028   Railroadiana; the collector's guide to
          railroad memorabilia.   N.Y.,Funk &
          Wagnalls,1976.
             274 p. ill.   10.95

RAILROADIANA

Previous Books by Charles Klamkin

If It Doesn't Work, Read the Instructions

*Barns: Their History,
Preservation and Restoration*

How to Buy Major Appliances

Weather Vanes, an American Folk Art

with Marian Klamkin

*Woodcarvings: North American
Folk Sculptures*

*Investing in Antiques and Popular Collectibles
for Pleasure and Profit*

RAILROADIANA

The Collector's Guide to Railroad Memorabilia

by CHARLES KLAMKIN

Funk & Wagnalls   NEW YORK

Designed by Ingrid Beckmen

Manufactured in the United States of America

Library of Congress Cataloging in Publication Data

Klamkin, Charles.
    Railroadiana.

    1. Railroads—Equipment and supplies—Collectors and collecting.
I. Title.
TF347.K48   625.1′0028   75-26977
ISBN 0-308-10221-5

10 9 8 7 6 5 4 3 2 1

Pardon me, Boy.

This is Lynn Klamkin's dedication.

Acknowledgments

I HAVE often found that those who own the finest collections and are the most knowledgeable are also the most generous in sharing their time and expertise with a researcher. This was especially true with this book where I have had access to the outstanding collection of railroadiana belonging to Fred Arone and John Martin, proprietors of the Depot Attic in Dobbs Ferry, New York.

Mr. Louis Goodwin, one of this country's preeminent timetable and postcard collectors, has also kindly allowed me to photograph important items from a collection built up over the course of sixty years.

The help, enthusiasm, and advice of these three men have aided immeasurably in the preparation and completion of this project.

Contents

RAILROADIANA

I

Introduction

T<small>HE RAILROAD</small>, second only to religion, has been the greatest civilizing and enlightening force in the world." That quotation is from Frank Munsey's editorial in the first issue of the *Railroad Man's Magazine*, published in October 1906, and it might well be argued that many a railroad enthusiast sometimes feels that God comes in second. Very few historical or collecting pursuits can boast of a larger number of thoroughly dedicated, knowledgeable buffs and collectors.

The history of railroading and the collecting of its artifacts are rooted in the "civilizing and enlightening" impact that interest in this form of transportation has had on the world's expansion and development. Particularly in North America, the railroads opened up vast territories of the continent to settlement and commerce, and more than any other factor caused both the United States and Canada to become great world powers.

Aside from their historical aspect, railroads are fascinating from the mechanical viewpoint. After the first primitive equipment was introduced barely one hundred and fifty years ago, railroads rapidly stimulated the finest engineering and innovative minds to produce

THE RAILROAD MAN'S MAGAZINE

Vol. I. OCTOBER, 1906. No. 1.

Just a Word About This New Magazine

BY MR. MUNSEY.

Message from the publisher in the first issue of the *Railroad Man's Magazine*, October, 1906.

THE railroad, second only to religion, has been the greatest civilizing and enlightening force in the world. It has eliminated space and brought backwoods sections in touch with the polish and alertness of the cities. In conjunction with the telegraph, it has daily placed the news of the world before the farmer and mechanic in the once remote places of the country. It has built up the great West—a region which was a limitless waste when this country was born, and which would still be a vast, uninhabited tract of barren prairie but for the railroad. It has stretched out from the little hamlets along the seaboard and created an empire the like of which does not exist in the Old World.

With a population to-day of well-nigh ninety millions, the United States owes perhaps fifty millions to the railroad, without which our development would have been confined to the Atlantic coast. We should have had no way of bringing grain and cattle from the West, no way of transporting coal from the mines and iron ore to the furnaces, or of carrying the finished product to the centers of trade. Gold and silver and copper would still largely be locked up in the recesses of the mountains.

But the material development brought about by the railroad is not the

thousands of original inventions and refinements. It is perhaps this preoccupation with history, nostalgia, and mechanics that makes the collecting of railroad-related items, or railroadiana, so rewarding.

One of the prerequisites if any collecting hobby is to be popular is, of course, availability of material; another is its scope and range. In both respects railroadiana fills the bill admirably. As pointed out, railroads have been around for about a century and a half and were huge enterprises affecting and penetrating every section of the continent from the most remote whistle-stop to the great urban centers. Every depot, freightyard, agent's office, each piece of rolling stock, and even every mile of track can yield something of interest to the collector.

Within the framework of railroadiana can be included mechanical devices, such as locks and keys, lanterns, engine bells, whistles, and headlights; communication equipment, such as telegraph and telephone items, and ticket punches and validators. An especially prestigious collector's item is the builder's plate that was affixed to each steam, electric, or diesel locomotive when it left its builder's manufacturing shop. These, to be sure, are rather sad artifacts when thought of in terms of the mounted heads of the big-game hunter. Just as we know that the splendid animal specimen now hanging on the wall as a trophy is dead, so a builder's plate in a display cabinet represents a great engine that has long since gone to the scrapyard.

Other collectibles would include the caps, badges, and buttons worn by railroad personnel, indicating their position and the lines for which they worked. The object in collecting this category, as in most other railroadiana, is to secure the widest possible representation of railroad companies both active and defunct. The badges, which identified jobs from baggagemaster to brakeman, were worn by almost all operating railroad men while the uniform buttons were confined mostly to conductors.

The dining cars once provided a mother lode of useful and distinctive collectibles. Railroad china, silverware, and linens are

A brass plate identifying the builder is attached to each locomotive before it leaves the shop where it was made. These are two fairly rare builder's plates. More common would be those from the Baldwin or American Locomotive Works.

reminiscent of the days of gracious dining on the great passenger trains when a five- or seven-course meal could be purchased for as little as a dollar. The most desirable of these plates, cups, saucers, knives, forks, spoons, serving pieces, tablecloths, and napkins are marked with the names, monograms, or insignia of the railroads that owned them. Some collectors endeavor to round up a complete dinner service from a single rail line while others try to secure the broadest selection from many roads. The collector with status in this area is able to serve his guests a complete meal using only pieces from his Santa Fe or New York Central services. Even more impressive is the collector who can do this with pieces from a railroad that went out of business years ago or has discontinued its passenger and dining-car operations.

The broadest area among railroad collectibles and the one that offers the widest range of interest is paper ephemera. So much of a railroad's history, promotion, and day-to-day operations was recorded on paper in one form or another that this field is practically endless. First in importance in the paper category are, unquestionably, timetables. Timetables seem to have a romance and a mystique all their own. Collectors who can ignore a complete set of ninety-year-old B & O buttons or a builder's plate from a 1906 Baldwin steam locomotive will travel thousands of miles and pay hundreds of dollars for a timetable from the Durango and Silver Creek Railroad or some other equally obscure and long-forgotten Colorado narrow-gauge mining railroad.

Purists in the timetable department may confine or augment their collections by seeking not only timetables issued to the public but those that the railroads printed expressly for their own employees. While not as colorful or artistically designed as those printed to promote passenger traffic, the employee timetables are far more detailed and precise, and provide a great deal more information as to actual railroad operations.

Associated with timetables are the posters or handbills announcing railroad schedules, special excursions, or advising of schedule changes. Some of these are very attractive, and when framed and hung on the wall, provide a decorative note to a railroadiana collector's home or office.

Vying with timetables in the degree of collector enthusiasm are annual passes. These passes, about the size of our present-day credit cards, were issued by all railroads and entitled the named bearer, and sometimes his family as well, to free passage over the rails of the issuing company for the period of a year. They were given not only to employees, but as a courtesy to executives of other railroads and as a form of bribery to politicians and others of influence whose goodwill the railroads might wish to enjoy. In the acquisition of annual passes, the emphasis ranges from the obscurity of the issuing railroad to the importance of either the person to whom the pass was issued or the railroad mogul who signed it.

Other paper collectibles are passenger tickets, train orders advising engineers of changes in their scheduled destination or mode of operation, advertising posters and calendars, railroad employees' rule books, promotional literature, dining-car menus, postcards, and photographs. All these areas, except photographs, will be discussed more fully in later chapters. Contemporary photographs of old, long-gone trains, railroad stations, and trainmen are highly prized by a great many collectors. This field, however, is so vast that literally hundreds of books with such pictures have been published, ranging from general surveys to such highly specialized subjects as the railroads serving the Hawaiian sugarcane industry or North Carolina logging camps.

There are innumerable adjunct collectibles associated with railroads and railroading that include such advertising or souvenir items as ashtrays, paperweights, playing cards, and folders describing the luxuries and amenities of the Twentieth Century Limited, the Super Chief, or other "name" trains. Indeed practically anything relating to railroading in any context is collectible. In this miscellaneous group belong books, magazines, and even sheet music if the song is associated with railroading or if there is a picture of a train on the cover. Phonograph records of railroad songs or railroad sounds, especially in stereo, are also collected.

Among the great number of railroad fans, there is a smaller group whose interest is taken up almost exclusively by old trolley lines. They collect anything having to do with the old electrified inter- and intraurban lines that have now become almost extinct. Among the collectibles in this specialty are timetables, photographs, postcards, motormen and conductors' badges, mechanical devices pertaining to the trolleys, and in some cases, the trolley cars themselves. There are some collectors who confine their efforts to the history and development of a single trolley line and others who specialize in the transit system of a particular city or district. This latter group comprises those who collect memorabilia from New York City subways, San Francisco cable cars, or artifacts from the Boston, Chicago, Philadelphia, or any of a multitude of other local mass-transit facilities.

This virtually endless supply and variety of material is one of the reasons that the collection of railroadiana has become so widespread. As in any collecting hobby or business, there are scarce or rare items that command high prices. But no matter how fascinating or desirable a collecting hobby may be, it will soon lose its popularity if collectors become discouraged due to limited availability of objects and prohibitive expense. This is not yet the case in regard to railroadiana. There is a broad enough choice among specialties and a large enough reservoir of individual items still available to make the pursuit rewarding.

There are thousands of collectors seeking to acquire railroadiana in one or more specific areas and others just as numerous trying to collect anything that is railroad-related. Who are these collectors, why do they collect, and how are they able to augment their collections?

A recent one-day show and sale of railroadiana held in a western Connecticut city attracted collectors not only from adjacent states but from as far away as Pennsylvania, Virginia, Iowa, and even Ontario, Canada. A New Jersey collectors' club chartered a bus, so that its members could share expenses and travel in comfort. This also gave the New Jersey group the additional opportunity to sell and swap among themselves during the three-hour trip.

A cross-section of the regular occupations of the collectors attending this meeting found lawyers, real-estate salesmen, active and retired railroad employees, housewives, a homicide detective, and high school teen-agers. All of them were actively engaged in buying, selling, swapping railroadiana and trading information on all facets of the hobby. What was most remarkable was the depth of knowledge these collectors displayed in respect to old, long-forgotten railroad companies and operations. They knew when they flourished, where they ran, the kind of equipment and rolling stock that was used, and when they went out of business or were taken over and absorbed into another railroad system.

One of the reasons these people were so familiar with the background of their hobby was that many of them grew up in railroading. Some still worked for the railroads while many were sons and daughters of railroad men. Many of those who had no family tie had been raised in towns where the railroad was the chief industry, the major employer, and the focus of the entire economic life of the community. Other collectors with no particular exposure to railroading by virtue of heritage or environment had been caught up in the railroad mystique, and become just as informed and enthusiastic as though they had grown up with the sound of the train whistle coming in their windows.

Methods of collecting railroadiana can vary from the traditional to the clandestine. The most direct avenue open to collectors is to buy from the recognized dealers in this specialty. Although there is a sizable number of individuals trading in railroadiana, most of them do this on a part-time basis; they operate out of homes, basements, and garages and are seen only at shows. There are a few dealers, however, with whom the buying and selling of railroad collectibles is a full-time occupation. They own stores, maintain warehouses, and conduct an active mail-order business by publishing a catalog issued on a fairly regular schedule. These larger dealers advertise in many of the general collecting journals, such as the *Antiques Trader*, and in most of the specialized railroading magazines. There are only a handful of such enterprises that might be called railroadiana supermarkets. Although they can be found on the East Coast, in the Middle West, and the Far West, they are too few to be accessible to most of the collectors who would like to visit them in person.

This means that perhaps as much as three quarters of an important dealer's business is carried on by mail. Collectors frequently advise these dealers of their specific wants or make them aware of a general area of interest. When a dealer acquires an item he knows to be of interest to a certain collector, he will write to him and furnish a description and price quotation. This is the advantage of doing business with an active dealer-specialist. He is constantly buying material whenever he can find it and wherever it is offered. His job is simplified if he knows just what his customers are looking for.

A great deal of inventory must be bought by these dealers purely on speculation. If a dealer learns that a railroad—or more frequently these days, its trustee in bankruptcy—is planning to dispose of some property, he must be prepared to enter a substantial bid for its acquisition. This may result in his buying a railroad's entire dining-car china or silver service or the contents of an almost forgotten storeroom full of old timetables, posters, promotional folders, and calendars. These purchases represent a substantial investment, and it may be several years before they can be entirely liquidated and a profit realized.

One sale at which dealers did not fare too well was held within the past few years by the trustees of the Penn Central Railroad. It was decided to auction off surplus or obsolete equipment at its Thirtieth Street Station in Philadelphia. The sale attracted not only dealers and collectors from all parts of the country but wealthy nostalgia buffs as well. This latter group bid up the price of most items to levels far beyond what collectors of railroadiana were accustomed to pay. The few dealers who did plunge have found that currently they have been unable to sell at a profit the merchandise bought at the Penn Central auction.

Aside from dealers, a great deal of railroadiana is acquired from retired railroad employees, or from their estates if they are deceased. Buttons, badges, passes, employee timetables and rule books, lanterns and switch keys, are typical of the items that can be collected from this resource. Quite often pieces of railroad property turn up among an employee's effects that were never intended for individual use and were obviously appropriated at some time in an unauthorized manner. This would include operating equipment, such as switch lamps, communications devices, passenger-car lighting devices and other appurtenances, and almost anything else that could manage to disappear from a railroad's operating equipment or offices. This is a very strong reason why prudent railroad personnel executives have long had a distinct bias against hiring railroad buffs.

As in many collecting hobbies a great deal of trading takes place among railroadiana devotees. This is one of the best and cheapest ways of upgrading a collection, weeding out duplicates, and making contact with other collectors. At club meetings, shows, and sales a lot of material can change hands with very little cash in evidence. Swapping four recent Southern Railway timetables for one vintage New York Central is in the best tradition of Yankee horse trading.

Railroadiana has all the attributes of a worthwhile collecting pastime. It incorporates history, nostalgia, invention, and preservation; it can be used decoratively or usefully and has a definite potential for appreciation in value. It gives the collector, also, the opportunity to meet a lot of other people who are as crazy about the subject as he.

2

Timetables and Schedules

As a railroad collectible, timetables rank very high in terms of desirability, status, and number of collectors. Among the reasons for their popularity is the fact that there is still an ample supply left to choose from. Except for a relatively small number of distinct rarities, most dealers can allow a browser to riffle through boxes and bins of hundreds and hundreds of timetables. The modest prices and wide selection of rail lines available are somewhat surprising considering that many of these items are from fifty to seventy-five years old. Lots of timetables from the 1950's or later can be bought for as little as a quarter, while most of the older ones sell for only one or two dollars.

In addition to supply, we should bear in mind that very few other railroad collectibles provide as much information about the day-to-day passenger operations of a railroad. The timetable reveals the line's route, the communities it served, and the frequency of service, which indicates the level of activity at the time it was in effect. All this lore is contained very compactly and can be easily stored or attractively displayed.

Some collectors ignore the more expensive items and concentrate on acquiring only timetables from a single railroad. Usually this is a line that served the area in which the collector grew up or now lives. His object is to gather as complete a series as possible, with the ultimate aim of owning every timetable the railroad issued during the period it was in business. This pursuit may not be too expensive as it is unlikely that too many other collectors will share an identical passion. But it can be time-consuming, especially if the railroad operated for fifty years and has merged or gone out of business within the past twenty years or so.

Collectors in this category sometimes exhibit remarkable loyalty and tenacity of purpose. For example, a collector recently asked a major eastern dealer if he had any timetables of the Long Island Rail Road. The Long Island, which serves thousands of commuters daily, carrying them in and out of New York City, has had a long history of mechanical, operating, and labor problems and has been a constant source of irritation and frustration to its patrons. Nevertheless this collector, who had suffered the L.I.R.R.'s eccentricities of service for many years, could not be interested in any other timetables.

Among the real prizes in collectible timetables are those issued in the late nineteenth century by some of the small, narrow-gauge railroads serving the mining camps of Colorado. For the most part, these routes were in existence only from the time they were built until the diggings in any particular area gave out. The names of the railroads and the towns they served are redolent with the romance of the Old West. The Durango and Silver Creek and the Florence and Cripple Creek in Colorado and the White Pass and Yukon in Alaska are a few of these. The only railroad still in existence that came into being during the mining boom in the Rocky Mountain states is the Denver and Rio Grande Western.

Also highly desirable are early examples of fine color printing, which was coming into vogue around the turn of the century. Some of the highly prized timetables in this category are those issued by the Colorado Midland Railway, the Kansas City Southern Railway, the California Northwestern Railway, and the Hannibal and St. Joseph Rail Road.

The earliest timetables were not the elaborately detailed folders we are familiar with but were simple listings either published in local

Timetables from the long-forgotten railroads that served the mining camps in Colorado, Nevada and Alaska are among the most sought-after collector's items.

Time Table and Connections.

Colorado Midland

RAILROAD.

July, '95, Edition.

GEO. W. RISTINE,
Receiver and General Manager.

W. F. BAILEY,
General Passenger Agent.

GENERAL OFFICES, DENVER, COLORADO.

6-12-40m.   RAND, McNALLY & CO., PRINTERS, CHICAGO.

SUMMER SEASON, 1899

COLORADO AND NORTHWESTERN RAILWAY

THE SWITZERLAND TRAIL OF AMERICA

C & N RY.

J. T. BLAIR, General Manager, Boulder, Colo.

For further information, Excursion
Rates, etc., call on or address M. M. MAYS, City Passenger Agent,
217 Cooper Building, Denver, Colorado.

TONOPAH & TIDEWATER COMPANY

I & I

THE NEVADA SHORT LINE

TO
RHYOLITE
BEATTY
SPRINGDALE
BONNIE CLARE
GOLDFIELD
TONOPAH
BLAIR JUNCTION

M. SMITH, President   JOHN RYAN, General Manager
C. B. ZABRISKIE, Secretary and Treasurer
W. R. ALBERGER, Traffic Manager, LOS ANGELES

the
White Pass & Yukon Route

WHITE PASS & YUKON ROUTE
GATEWAY TO THE YUKON

To the
ATLIN
YUKON
KLONDIKE
and
WHITE
HORSE
Mining
Districts

A. B. NEWELL, Vice-Pres. & Gen. Mgr.
Seattle, Wash. and Skaguay, Alaska
J. FRANCIS LEE, Traffic Manager
Seattle, Wash. and Skaguay, Alaska

SPECIAL TIME TABLE.

LIEUT. GEN. GRANT'S TRAIN

MILWAUKEE TO CHICAGO.

TUESDAY, SEPTEMBER 5th, 1865.

FOR THIS DAY ONLY.

Leave Milwaukee	8.50 A. M.
Arrive Racine	9.35 "
Leave Racine Junction	10.15 "
Arrive Kenosha	10.38 "
Leave Kenosha	10.45 "
Leave State Line	meet No. 1. 11.06 "
Arrive Waukegan	11.26 "
Leave Waukegan	11.32 "
Leave Rockland	11.42 "
Leave Lake Forest	11.46 "
Leave Highland Park	11.55 "
Leave Glencoe	12.03 P. M.
Leave Winetka	12.08 "
Leave Evanston	12.18 "
Leave Rosehill	12.26 "
Arrive Chicago	12.50 "

This Special Train, as against Train No. 1, will have the right to the Road, for thirty-five (35) minutes beyond its own time to run to any Station, if Train No. 1 has failed to arrive; and Train No. 1 will have the right to the Road, to run from any Station after waiting thirty-five (35) minutes beyond the time of this Special Train, keeping thirty-five (35) minutes behind its own time, until this Special Train is passed.

All other Trains will keep entirely out of the way of this Special Train.

This Special Train will stop only at Racine, Racine Junction, Kenosha, State Line and Waukegan.

Train No. 1 will side track at State Line.

GEO. L. DUNLAP, General Superintendent.

C. C. WHEELER, Superintendent.

An 1865 timetable with very strong historical associations. The train conveying General Grant was given special clearance for the four-hour trip between Milwaukee and Chicago.

newspapers or printed as handbills or posters. By 1880 the railroads had expanded so rapidly that more complicated timetables were required to schedule the greatly increased traffic and provide for the accommodation of passengers using the connecting lines needed to get to their destinations. The concern that progressive railroad men had for the artistic appeal and technical accuracy of their line's timetables is pointed up in the following quotation. It is an excerpt from a chapter in *The American Railway* published by Charles

Single-sheet timetables, which were posted at the depots and not given away, are somewhat scarcer than passenger timetables.

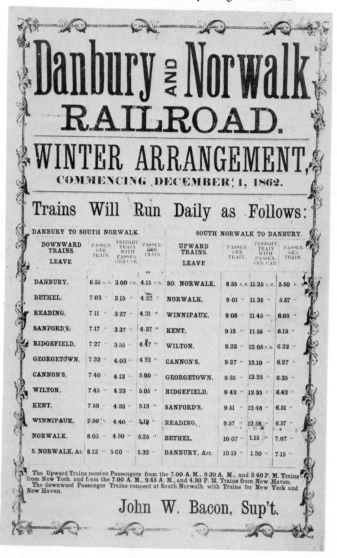

NEW YORK CENTRAL

"AMERICA'S GREATEST RAILWAY SYSTEM."

& HUDSON RIVER R. R.

Hudson-Fulton Celebration.

REDUCED FARES to

NEW YORK CITY

ALSO

TROY AND ALBANY

Schedule of Fares.

STATION.	New York.	Troy or Albany.	STATION.	New York.	Troy or Albany.
Middleville	$7.50	$1.90	Horseshoe	$11.05	$4.25
Newport	7.65	2.00	Childwold	11.35	4.45
Poland	7.80	2.10	Piercefield	11.40	4.50
Prospect Jct.	8.10	2.30	Tupper Lake Jct.	11.55	4.60
Hinckley	8.25	2.40	Saranac Inn	12.15	5.00
Forestport	8.65	2.65	Lake Clear Jct.	12.25	5.05
White Lake	8.95	2.85	Saranac Lake	12.45	5.20
McKeever	9.15	3.00	Gabriels	12.45	5.20
Fulton Chain	9.45	3.20	Rainbow Lake	12.45	5.20
Clearwater	9.70	3.35	Lake Kushaqua	12.45	5.20
Big Moose	9.90	3.50	Loon Lake	12.45	5.20
Beaver River	10.20	3.70	Mountain View	13.30	5.75
Nehasane	10.60	3.95	Owl's Head	13.45	5.85
Long Lake, West	10.90	4.15	Malone	13.80	6.10
Lake Placid			$12.90		$5.50.

Dates of Sale. To New York September 24th to October 2nd inclusive. To Troy and Albany, October 7th, 8th and 9th.

Final Return Limit on all Tickets October 10th.

Excursion Tickets. At fares shown above will be on sale to New York, also to Albany and Troy for all regular trains of dates shown herein and tickets to all points will bear final return limit of Sunday, October 10th. These tickets will be good in Pullman parlor or sleeping cars but will not be good on "Empire State Express" or other Limited Trains. Baggage may be checked thereon.

PROGRAM OF THE CELEBRATION.

SATURDAY, Sept. 25th—Naval Parade encircling fleet of war vessels including the "Clermont" and "Half Moon".
ILLUMINATED PARADE IN EVENING AND DECORATION OF FLEET.
SUNDAY, Sept. 26th—Religious services and ceremonies.
MONDAY, Sept. 27th—Dedication of Henry Hudson Monument.
TUESDAY, Sept. 28th—Historical Parade and Pageant participated in by all nationalities, procession of floats and tableaux.
WEDNESDAY, Sept. 29th—Aquatic Sports, Riverside Park, etc.
THURSDAY, Sept. 30th—Grand Military Parade by U. S. Army, Naval and Marine Corps, National Guard, etc.
FRIDAY, Oct. 1st—Grand Naval Parade to Newburgh.
SATURDAY, Oct. 2d—Carnival Parade in Manhattan—50 Illuminated Floats, escorted by various organizations.

Special Observation Train. Arrangements have been made for accommodation of persons desiring to witness naval parade on Saturday, September 25th only, for Special Observation Train to be located on New York Central tracks opposite Riverside Park, train being ready for occupancy at 10:00 a. m., from West 108th Street to West 116th Street. This observation train will consist of flat cars with seats erected thereon and is **Entirely Covered With Canvas Canopy Affording Unobstructed View.**

Tickets for seats on this Special Observation Train can be obtained upon early application to Ticket Agents, N. Y. C. Lines. **Price, $2.00.**

J. F. FAIRLAMB,
General Passenger Agent, New York.

C. HARTIGAN,
General Agent, Montreal, Que.

Form 81 C. H. 9-14-00-15M. O.M.S.

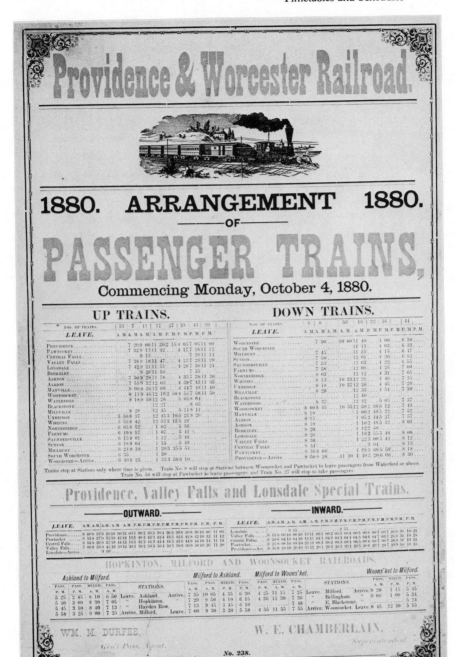

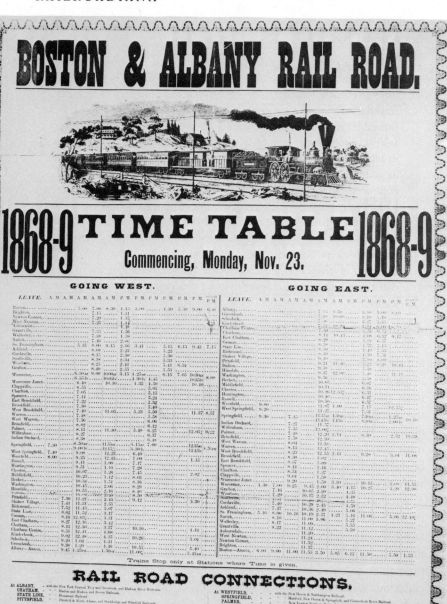

Scribner's Sons in 1893 and was written by a vice-president of the Long Island Rail Road:

> When a railroad company takes up the question of timetables, it has a matter of importance to handle which on many roads receives very little attention. When the passenger traffic is heavy, the number of travellers during the year running into the millions, the demand for timetables is very large. This refers directly to the time-table sheets or folders, which every company must keep on hand at its stations, and in other public places and hotels, for the convenience of the traveller, in addition to the printed schedules which are framed and hung up conspicuously on the walls of its waiting-rooms. A neat and attractive folder for general circulation is very desirable, particularly if competition is very strong. There is more virtue in a neatly made up schedule of trains than one would suppose. One in doubt is apt to reason that the road is kept up in corresponding condition, and that the trains are made up on the same plan, and consequently would prefer to go by that route rather than by one whose trains were advertised on cheap leaflets.

The logistics involved in compiling a timetable for a good-sized railroad are truly formidable. Among the factors to be considered are the peak times of passenger traffic density, the availability of the proper type and quantity of equipment, and the speeds at which it must travel. Whether a route is single- or double-tracked is also of the utmost importance, for if trains can not pass each other in opposite directions, the points at which they must be sidetracked must also be computed. Express, local, and baggage service have to be factored in, as well as where freight operations might conflict with passenger service.

Around 1880, timetables of the type issued to the public had evolved from a simple card to the more complex folders we are familiar with today. Some railroads continued to have them printed in an austere black and white style, while others began using their timetables to carry an advertising message. The more promotion-conscious railroads would use some of the space to extol the luxury and safety of their equipment, the speed of their service, or the natural beauty of the scenery along the route.

One of the most highly prized timetables is that of the Hannibal and St. Joseph Rail Road issued in 1879. The cover is typical of the period and employs about ten different type faces to announce that

A group of nineteenth-century timetables from railroads serving the northeastern part of the United States.

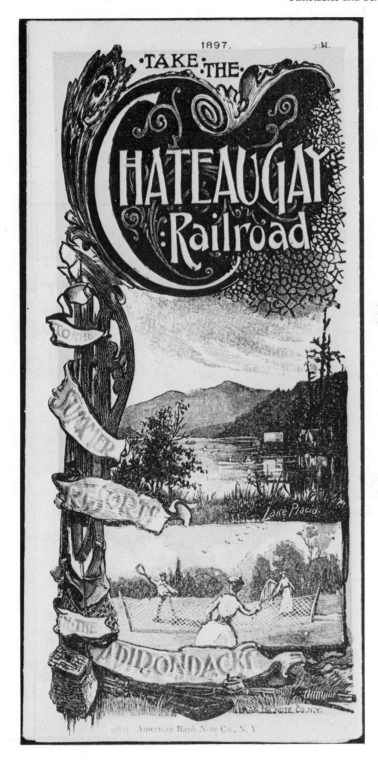

In this group of timetables from southern railroads, the Florida lines were featuring travel through that state's orange groves as early as 1888.

30

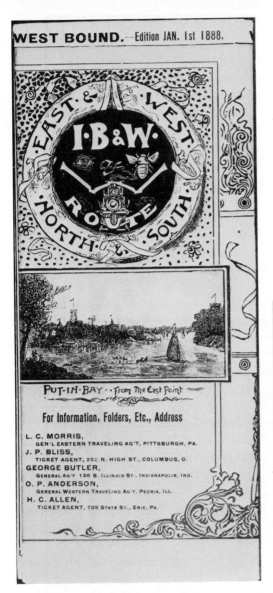

Three midwestern railroad timetables dating from the last decade of the nineteenth century. The Indiana, Illinois and Iowa Rail Road and the Indianapolis, Bloomington and Western used a rebus in their corporate trademarks.

this is "The Old Reliable Route to the West." The timetable unfolds to display a 4-4-0 locomotive with wood-carrying tender, mail and baggage car, and three passenger cars passing over a stone viaduct. The light from the engine's headlamp is shown as a bright white cone on which is printed "The New Electric Headlamp." Superimposed above the train is the legend in a flowing script, "Always on Time." Beneath this upper half of the timetable is a map of the portion of the United States extending from the East Coast to as far west as the states of Colorado and Wyoming. On this map is indicated the line's prime route across the state of Missouri from Hannibal on the Mississippi River westward to St. Joseph with a spur going south to Kansas City. It also shows how the Hannibal and St. Joseph connects with roads serving Detroit, Cincinnati, Chicago, St. Louis, and the West, presumably as far as the Pacific Ocean. Both these illustrations are printed in beautifully subdued shades of red, rust, yellow, and gray. This is true as well for one half of the reverse side of the unfolded sheet which depicts a cutaway view of the line's Horton "Reclining Chair Car." This car, which was a feature of the Hannibal and St. Joseph's passenger accommodations, was called to the traveler's attention on the front of the timetable as well as the fact that Pullman sleeping cars were also available.

Another series of sought-after timetables are those issued around the turn of the century by the Colorado and Midland Railway. This group depicts an American Indian warrior of the western plains; on the 1899 timetable he is shown standing with shield and spear while on the 1900 and 1903 editions he is mounted on horseback. In all three cases the line's logo with the legend "Pike's Peak Route" is emblazoned on his shield. The quality of the color reproduction is excellent on all of them, but the two later examples of 1900 and 1903 are distinguished by a double-page color spread with scenic backgrounds. The November 1900 copy shows the Indian watching a train making its way along a gorge, and the October 1903 edition has him superimposed on a view of Mount Sopris, Colorado.

Also desired by collectors is a group of timetables published in 1903 by the Kansas City Southern Railway Company. Some of these display a black crow to emphasize the company's slogan, spelled out in a panel on the cover, "Straight as the Crow Flies," while an adjacent panel describes the route, "Kansas City to the

Gulf." A variation issued in February 1901 shows a lighthouse at Port Arthur, Texas, which was the southern terminus of the line and named for Arthur Stillwell, the founder of the K.C.S.

Two timetables issued by the Carolina Clinchfield and Ohio Railway are of special interest to collectors. The line was quite small and was not in business long. Only two of its timetables are known to have been published with color lithographed covers. They depict scenes along the line's route, which made its way through some of the most scenic parts of the Appalachian Mountains.

A distinct rarity is the boldly colored cover of the timetable of the Keokuk and Western Railroad Company with an illustration of a fierce-looking Chief Keokuk on the cover. Although the timetable indicates that this railroad served Kansas City, Des Moines, Omaha, Atchison, St. Joseph, and St. Louis, very little is known of its history, and this timetable may be the only example extant.

A diversified collection of the more unusual early timetables with good colored art work might include items from Mexico, Cuba, and Canada. Some collectors' interests extend beyond the North American continent, and they seek timetables in this category from South America, Europe, and elsewhere.

The timetables of most of America's long-departed electric street railways, or trolleys, have their own group of dedicated collectors. Once a common fixture in the life of almost every community, the interurban trolley lines rapidly gave way to the bus and the private automobile. For years the trolleys, especially those linking large and small towns, published timetables that were thrown away as soon as a new schedule superseded it. Now these old street railway timetables are actively collected, and the rarer items have as much prestige as those from the more obscure steam railroads.

Two scarce timetables are those issued by the New Bedford and Onset Street Railway Company and the Connecticut Valley Electric Transit Route. Both are unusual in that they are in color, and both have an illustration of a young woman on the cover. The New Bedford lady is in a red dress and is shown holding a pulley connected to an overhead trolley cable along which she is traveling. The fashionably dressed woman on the Connecticut Valley cover is carrying a parasol in her right hand while under her left arm is tucked an early open-sided trolley car. In respect to trolley cars a postcard illustrated in this book shows a trolley line, the Illinois

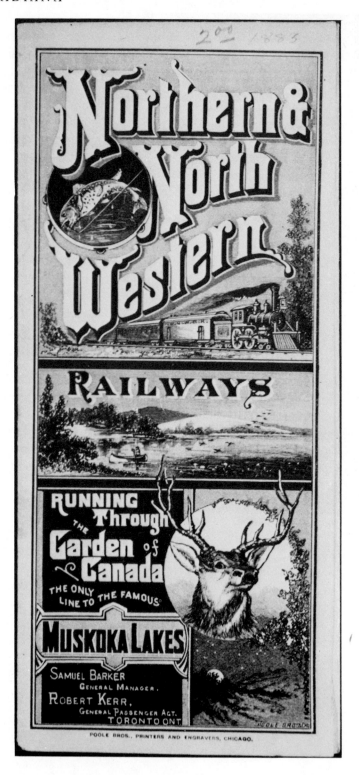

The covers of some early Canadian railroad timetables featured illustrations of some of that country's wildlife.

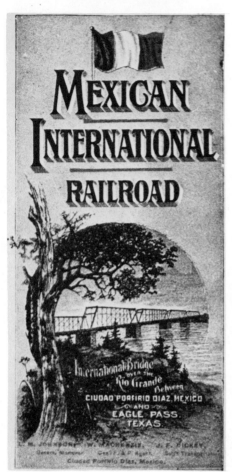

Early timetables from Cuba, Mexico, and Canada are also of interest to the collector.

The only Railway affording Passengers a full view of the Falls.

W. H. HURLBURT,
Gen'l Pass. and Ticket Ag't.

W. P. TAYLOR,
Gen'l Manager.

J. W. REYNOLDS, General Eastern Passenger Agent,
409 Broadway, New York.

N. E.   Matthews, Northrup & Co., "Morning Express" Printing House, Buffalo, N. Y.

PHILADELPHIA
AND
WEST CHESTER
TRACTION CO.

TIME TABLE

DAILY and SUNDAY

TRAINS BETWEEN

PHILADELPHIA (69th St. Terminal)

AND

Newtown Square—West Chester
Highland Park—Llanerch—Brookline—Ardmore
Clifton—Aldan—Collingdale—Sharon Hill
Drexel Hill—Springfield—Media

During rush hours and on Saturdays, Sundays and Holidays, additional trains will be run when necessary.

Trains stop only on signal at points designated by signs reading "CAR STOP" and stations. Signal should be given by passenger distinctly and in ample time for motorman to stop train at landing.

The connections shown are given for the benefit of patrons, but this Company will not be responsible for connections, errors or changes.

SCHEDULE IN EFFECT JANUARY 5, 1931

SUBJECT TO CHANGE WITHOUT NOTICE

Trolley-line and interurban railway timetables attract both specialist and general collectors.

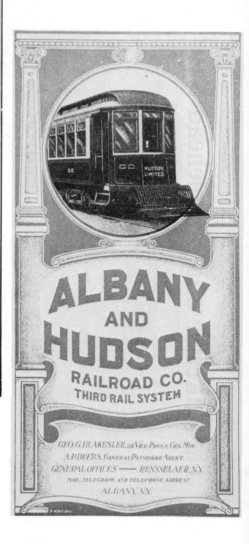

The Lakeside and Marblehead Railroad Company

TIME TABLE NO. 47

Eastern Standard Time

	3	1	STATIONS		2	4
	P. M.	A. M.			A. M.	P. M.
Lv.	5:00	7:50	MARBLEHEAD	Ar.	9:35	6:09
	5:04	7:54	LAKESIDE		9:31	6:05
	5:12	8:01	PICCOLO		9:22	5:56
	5:16	8:06	VIOLET		9:18	5:52
Ar.	5:25	8:15	DANBURY	Lv.	9:10	5:44

Connections With New York Central Railroad at Danbury, Ohio

Train No. 1, leaving Lakeside at 7:54 a. m., makes direct connections with East and West bound New York Central trains arriving in Cleveland at 10:50 a. m. and Toledo at 10:25 a. m. Train No. 3, leaving Lakeside at 5:04 p. m., makes direct connection with New York Central west bound train arriving in Toledo at 7:30 p. m. Train No. 1, arriving in Toledo at 10:25 a. m., makes direct connection with Big Four Railway for Dayton and Cincinnati.

ALL TRAINS DAILY EXCEPT SUNDAY

For rates and other information ask local ticket agents or take up with

O. R. STURZINGER, Gen'l Supt., Marblehead, Ohio

J. G. YULE, Gen'l Mgr.,
1102 Leader-News Bldg.,
CLEVELAND, OHIO

O. F. GARDNER, Gen'l Frt. and Pass. Agt.
1102 Leader-News Bldg.,
CLEVELAND, OHIO

In this group of nineteenth-century timetables from railroads covering the western United States, the Chicago Rock Island and Pacific advertises connections to Australia, China, and Japan.

Traction System, which ran a trolley sleeping car between Peoria and St. Louis more than fifty years ago. This was a truly unusual function for a trolley car.

The type of timetable that appeals to the collector with a thorough background in railroading is the employee timetable. They are never as attractive or as lavishly produced as some of the passenger timetables, but these mundane-appearing folders contain the information required for the day-to-day operation of the railroad. The fact that they were not meant to be seen by the traveling public is evidenced by the legend appearing in bold type on the cover of practically every employee timetable, "For the Government and Information of Employees Only."

A collectible adjunct of employee timetables are the company rule books. Each railroad published its own set of rules, and although most of the regulations were standard, there were some rules peculiar to individual companies. One of these was the rule that the callboys hired to round up a train's crew were never to call an engineer, fireman, brakeman, or conductor out of a saloon. But the callboys soon learned that they could earn rather decent tips from the trainmen by ignoring that particular rule.

Some of the older of today's thousands of timetable collectors began their hobby as children years ago when the timetables were freely available in railroad depots, hotels, and other distribution points. Like many other items of paper ephemera having only a temporary useful value, timetables were usually thrown away when they went out of date, and only a relatively small portion of the millions that were printed have been saved. Among those that do remain are the few rare treasures and the many more numerous yet interesting and evocative examples that make their collecting a satisfying hobby.

COPPER RANGE RAILROAD CO.

TIME TABLE

No. 98

To take effect 12:01 A. M.
Sunday, Jan. 8, 1933

For the Government and Information of Employees Only

G. H. WESCOTT,   A. H. EHLERS,
General Manager   Superintendent

UNITED STATES RAILROAD ADMINISTRATION,
W. G. McADOO, Director General of Railroads

Toledo & Ohio Central Railroad

Time Table No. 58

To take effect at 12:01 a. m.

Sunday, Jan. 12th, 1919

Central Standard Time

For the Government and Information of Employes only

Destroy all previous issues.

H. E. SPEAKS,   C. L. GARDNER
General Superintendent.   Superintendent

I. B. CHADWICK,
Assistant Superintendent

51040

Railroads issue special timetables that are invariably marked "For the Government and Information of Employees Only." While not as attractive as passenger timetables, collectors prize them for their wealth of detailed information about railroad operations.

HOSPITAL DEPARTMENT

W. N. BLOUNT, M. D., Chief Surgeon, Laurel, Miss.

Mobile, Ala.	P. J. M. Acker ... Local Surgeon
Mobile, Ala.	S. H. Stephens ... Local Surgeon
Mobile, Ala.	J. C. O'Gwynn, Sr. ... Oculist
Mobile, Ala.	J. C. O'Gwynn, Jr. ... Oculist
Tuwn (Trichton), Ala.	A. M. Cowden ... Local Surgeon
Prichard, Ala.	J. R. Trimstead ... Local Surgeon
Lucedale, Miss.	J. A. Dorsett ... Local Surgeon
McLain, Miss.	Dan McLeod ... Local Surgeon
Beaumont, Miss.	F. J. Mathis ... Local Surgeon
Richton, Miss.	J. H. Newcombe ... Local Surgeon
Ovett, Miss.	F. McCarty ... Local Surgeon
Laurel, Miss.	Thos. R. Ramsey ... Local Surgeon
Laurel, Miss.	C. H. Ramsey ... Local Surgeon
Laurel, Miss.	J. C. Butler ... Local Surgeon
Laurel, Miss.	Jno. E. Green ... Local Surgeon
Laurel, Miss.	A. J. Carter ... Local Surgeon
Laurel, Miss.	W. S. Harper ... Oculist
Stringer, Miss.	A. M. Harrelson ... Local Surgeon
Bay Springs, Miss.	J. D. Thigpen ... Local Surgeon
Louin, Miss.	G. W. Land ... Local Surgeon
Montrose, Miss.	John V. James ... Local Surgeon
Newton, Miss.	Dudley Stevens ... Local Surgeon
Newton, Miss.	W. E. Rex ... Local Surgeon
Decatur, Miss.	S. R. Hinton ... Local Surgeon
Union, Miss.	Z. C. Hagan ... Local Surgeon
Union, Miss.	W. A. McMahon ... Local Surgeon
Decatur, Miss.	J. R. Plimmer ... Local Surgeon
Philadelphia, Miss.	W. J. Stribling ... Local Surgeon
Philadelphia, Miss.	W. R. Hand ... Local Surgeon
Noxapater, Miss.	F. F. Kilpatrick ... Local Surgeon
Louisville, Miss.	W. W. Parkes ... Local Surgeon
Louisville, Miss.	E. L. Richardson ... Local Surgeon
Louisville, Miss.	M. L. Montgomery ... Local Surgeon
Ackerman, Miss.	J. James ... Local Surgeon
Mathiston, Miss.	J. H. Bennan ... Local Surgeon
Maben, Miss.	W. B. Harpole ... Local Surgeon
Mantee, Miss.	B. K. Gore ... Local Surgeon
Houston, Miss.	J. R. Williams ... Local Surgeon
Houston, Miss.	J. R. Priest ... Local Surgeon
Houlka, Miss.	W. C. Walker ... Local Surgeon
Houlka, Miss.	J. H. Hood ... Oculist
Algoma, Miss.	J. G. Abernathy ... Local Surgeon
Pontotoc, Miss.	R. P. Donaldson ... Local Surgeon
Ecru, Miss.	J. B. Windham ... Local Surgeon
New Albany, Miss.	H. N. Mayer ... Local Surgeon
New Albany, Miss.	S. E. Eason ... Local Surgeon
Cotton Plant, Miss.	J. E. Pennebaker ... Local Surgeon
Blue Mountain, Miss.	Jas. I. Mayfield ... Local Surgeon
Ripley, Miss.	C. M. Murry ... Local Surgeon
Ripley, Miss.	R. M. Adams ... Local Surgeon
Falkner, Miss.	J. H. Pearce ... Local Surgeon
Brownfield, Miss.	R. S. Ford ... Local Surgeon
Middleton, Tenn.	J. A. Bowman ... Local Surgeon
Benoia, Tenn.	F. E. Whitlock ... Local Surgeon
Hornsby, Tenn.	W. L. Harben ... Local Surgeon
Silerton, Tenn.	W. H. Siler ... Local Surgeon
Jackson, Tenn.	W. C. Duckworth ... Local Surgeon
Jackson, Tenn.	R. D. White ... Local Surgeon
Jackson, Tenn.	J. T. Herron ... Oculist
Jackson, Tenn.	S. M. Herron ... Oculist
Eola, Tenn.	S. Farrow ... Local Surgeon
Alamo, Tenn.	C. G. Bowen ... Local Surgeon
Friendship, Tenn.	J. G. Carter ... Local Surgeon
Dyersburg, Tenn.	J. G. Price ... Local Surgeon
Paducah, Ky.	E. A. Jones ... Local Surgeon
Paducah, Ky.	W. P. Sights ... Local Surgeon
Meridian, Miss.	I. W. Cooper ... District Surgeon
Meridian, Miss.	H. R. Gully ... Local Surgeon
Meridian, Miss.	Leslie V. Rush ... Local Surgeon
Meridian, Miss.	G. Lamar Arrington ... Local Surgeon
Meridian, Miss.	A. G. Touchstone ... Oculist
Meridian, Miss.	H. Lowrey Rush ... Radiologist
Meridian, Miss.	R. R. Welch ... Consultant Neurologist
Schastopol, Miss.	W. F. Johnson ... Local Surgeon
Walnut Grove, Miss.	J. M. Golden ... Local Surgeon
Lena, Miss.	K. P. Wood ... Local Surgeon
Koch, Miss.	J. L. White ... Local Surgeon
Jackson, Miss.	Willis Walley ... Asst. Chief Surgeon
Jackson, Miss.	F. E. Werkheiser ... Local Surgeon
Jackson, Miss.	Jno. S. McIntosh ... Local Surgeon
Jackson, Miss.	J. G. Thompson ... Local Surgeon
Jackson, Miss.	Harvey F. Garrison, Jr. ... Local Surgeon
Jackson, Miss.	Harvey F. Garrison, Sr. ... Consultant Internist
Jackson, Miss.	Adas G. Wilde ... Oculist
Jackson, Miss.	Van Dyke Hagaman ... Oculist
Jackson, Miss.	Ross E. Anderson ... Oculist
Jackson, Miss.	J. S. Hickman ... Consultant Neurologist
Jackson, Miss.	C. A. Palmerlee ... Pathologist

LOCATION OF GENERAL HOSPITALS

Mobile, Ala.	City Hospital.
Mobile, Ala.	Mobile Infirmary.
Mobile, Ala.	Providence Infirmary.
Laurel, Miss.	Laurel General Hospital.

LOCATION OF EMERGENCY HOSPITALS

Newton, Miss.	Newton Sanitorium.
Houston, Miss.	Houston Hospital.
New Albany, Miss.	New Albany Hospital & Clinic.
New Albany, Miss.	Mayes Hospital.
Jackson, Tenn.	Memorial Hospital.
Jackson, Tenn.	Fitts White Clinic.
Dyersburg, Tenn.	The Baird-Brewer General Hospital.
Meridian, Miss.	Meridian Sanitarium.
Meridian, Miss.	Rush's Infirmary.
Jackson, Miss.	Willis Walley Hospital.
Jackson, Miss.	Baptist Hospital.

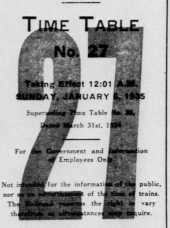

Gulf, Mobile and Northern R. R.

Alabama and Tennessee Divisions

TIME TABLE No. 27

Taking Effect 12:01 A.M.
SUNDAY, JANUARY 6, 1935

Superseding Time Table No. 26,
Dated March 31st, 1934

For the Government and Information
of Employees Only

Not intended for the information of the public,
nor as an advertisement of the time of trains.
The Railroad reserves the right to vary
therefrom as circumstances may require.

NOTE IMPORTANT CHANGES

P. E. ODELL, Vice-President

G. P. BROCK, General Manager

C. E. LANHAM, Superintendent Transportation

THE

WESTERN MARYLAND RAILWAY CO.

MIDDLE DIVISION

TIME TABLE No. 3

In Effect 12.01 A. M., Sunday, Nov. 16, 1913

EASTERN STANDARD TIME

FOR GOVERNMENT OF EMPLOYES ONLY

IMPORTANT CHANGES HAVE
BEEN MADE

A. H. MERRICK   F. L. BRENDEL
General Superintendent   Superintendent

New York and Putnam Railroad.

N. Y. C. & H. R. R. R. CO., Lessee.

Time Table No. 20.

FOR EMPLOYES ONLY.

++

Taking effect

Sunday, Nov. 15, 1903,

at 12.01 A.M.

STUDY the SPECIAL INSTRUCTIONS and
NOTE ALL CHANGES.

The Passenger Trains of this Company will
STOP ONLY to receive and discharge passengers at such stations as are designated
herein.

D. B. McCOY,

A. H. SMITH.

J. P. BRADFIELD.

C. F. SMITH.

THE GALVESTON, HARRISBURG & SAN ANTONIO RAILWAY COMPANY.

EL PASO DIVISION
— AND —
TEXAS & PACIFIC RAILWAY—RIO GRANDE DIVISION
BETWEEN EL PASO AND SIERRA BLANCA.

EMPLOYES' TIME TABLE

To Take Effect Wednesday, March 25th, 1914,

At 12:01 A. M. "Central Time."

At 12:01 A. M. "Mountain Time," Rio Grande and El Paso.

For the government and information of employes only, and not intended for the use of the public.
The Company reserves the right to vary from this Time Table at pleasure.

W. G. VAN VLECK,
Vice-President and General Manager.

G. S. WAID,
Assistant General Manager.

CHICAGO & NORTH-WESTERN RAILWAY

WISCONSIN DIVISION.

No. 202 **TIME TABLE** No. 202

Takes Effect Sunday, July 2, 1899,

The time on Passenger trains between Chicago and Baraboo has been reduced from that of previous schedule. Enginemen are expected to use good judgment in handling trains to this territory, and run fast at only such places as it is safe to do so, even though the schedule time is not made. In the elevated tracks an improved the possibilities are making, the time will also improve. All trains will approach white Macon carefully and not proceed until given proper signal by switch tender at that point. Knock signals will govern Wisconsin Division Trains and white signals will govern Milwaukee Division Trains.

AT 7:00 O'CLOCK, A. M.

The Interlocking Tower at Clybourn Junction has been taken down, and all trains, during elevation period, will come to a full stop for the railroad crossing and be governed by hand signals.

FOR THE GOVERNMENT AND INFORMATION OF EMPLOYES ONLY.

J. M. WHITMAN,
General Manager

S. SANBORN,
General Superintendent

W. A. GARDNER,
Ass't General Superintendent.

T. A. LAWSON,
Superintendent.

Railway guides, which incorporated the schedules of most of the U.S. railroads, were sold in great numbers in the nineteenth century and early twentieth century. The earliest issue, pictured here on the next page, is *Appleton's Guide* for September, 1864. All of these guides are collectible.

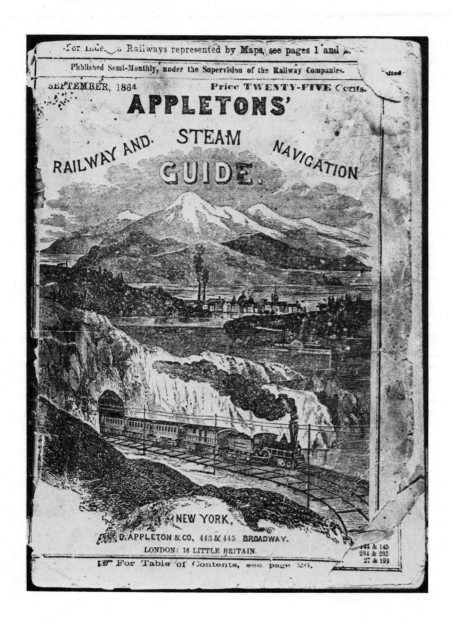

For Index o Railways represented by Maps, see pages 1 and 2.

Published Semi-Monthly, under the Supervision of the Railway Companies.

SEPTEMBER, 1864   Price TWENTY-FIVE Cents.

APPLETONS'

RAILWAY AND. STEAM NAVIGATION

GUIDE.

NEW YORK,
D. APPLETON & CO., 443 & 445 BROADWAY.
LONDON: 16 LITTLE BRITAIN.

For Table of Contents, see page 26.

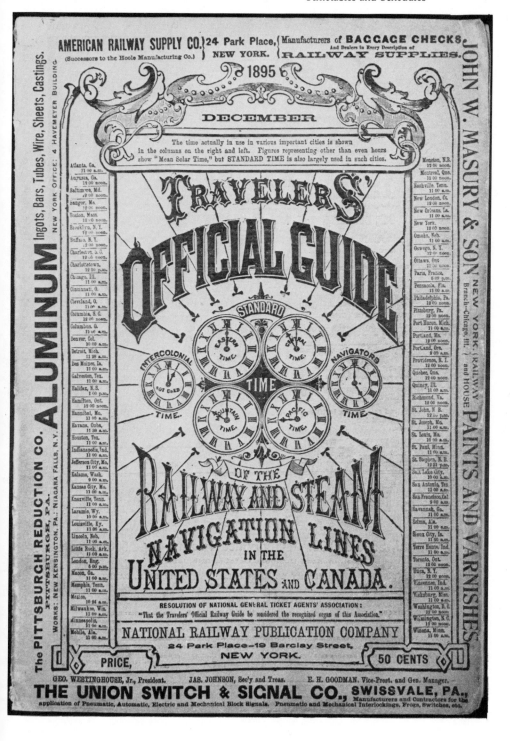

3

Lanterns, Switch Keys and Locks

L ANTERNS, signal lamps, and other lighting devices have been crucial items of railroad operating equipment from the days of the first steam trains right up to the present. As a collectible, lanterns are especially desirable because they go back so far in time that their development can be traced throughout the entire history of railroading. Also, lanterns can be identified as the property of specific railroads and collected with the goal of securing the widest representation of different lines.

The earliest lanterns used by railroads in the first half of the nineteenth century were of the common whale-oil variety with no special modification for railroad use. As the railroads grew, their need for a brighter, more dependable light became evident, and the kerosene-burning lantern was universally adopted. Since so many lanterns were required by even modest-sized railroads, it was economically feasible to have them made to a particular railroad's own specifications. This did not entail any revolutionary modification in design but generally just involved the identification on the lantern of the railroad which owned it. This was probably intended,

Early New York Central lantern.

also, to discourage pilferage of these highly useful and portable items that were a necessity for every household and farm.

The means by which the railroads identified a lantern as their property was by stamping the railroad's name on the metal part of the lantern and by having the name also embossed on the glass globe. The metal stamping was most frequently done on the flange, which covered the globe or chimney, but some lanterns have the road's name stamped on the metal base or fuel reservoir.

It is not difficult to find a great number of lanterns with the name of the railroad exhibited on the metal, but fewer are found with the raised lettering on the glass. Obviously this is because the glass, being more fragile, was subject to much breakage and replacement

A

B

C

Lanterns with the following railroad markings: A, Pere Marquette; B, New York, Ontario and Western; C, Central Vermont; D, Delaware and Hudson; E, New York Central; F, Erie.

D

E

F

Lantern with red glass globe and
Philadelphia and Reading Rail Road
markings.

during the time the lantern was in use. Owning an old lantern that
has the railroad's name on both the metal and the glass would tend to
indicate that it is original and not a restored or reproduction copy.
This is the kind of lantern the novice collector should look for, until
he learns which lanterns are acceptable with only the metal or the
glass suitably marked.

Some smaller railroads avoided the expense of having their names
stamped on the metal and were content to have only the glass
chimneys marked. Later, some of the bigger railroads continued to
purchase marked lanterns but supplied them to their personnel with
plain glass globes. By using commonly available stock lanterns or
globes, significant savings could be achieved.

Baltimore and Ohio lantern with railroad slogan "Safety First" embossed on red globe.

In addition to its railroad's initials being found on the globe, the Baltimore and Ohio Railroad included the slogan "Safety First" on some of the lantern globes used on the line. A much more unusual lantern, illustrated in this chapter, is the one on which is etched "G. Arnold/Conductor/G.T.R." The name, G. Arnold, is also stamped into the metal base. This lantern identified the user, his position, and the line for which he worked—the Grand Trunk Railway. The upper portion of the etched chimney is green glass, and the lower portion is clear. This is a distinctive collector's item from a railroad that has long since passed out of existence.

Railroads today have by and large abandoned the kerosene lanterns and now supply their workmen with the safer, more

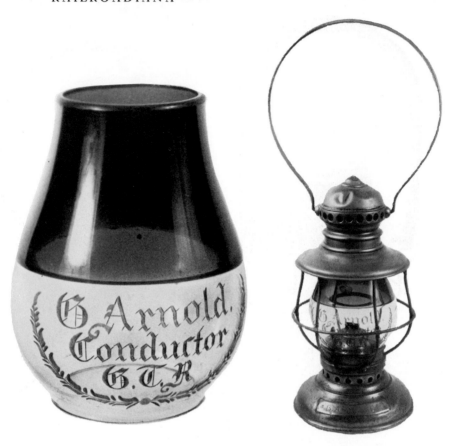

Lantern with green and clear glass globe was presented to a conductor on the Grand Trunk Railway upon his retirement. This type of presentation piece is particularly collectible.

compact, battery-powered electric models. This type is shown by an example indicating that it is the property of SPCO, or the Southern Pacific Company.

As in other areas of railroadiana, lanterns bearing the initials of defunct or merged railroads are the more sought-after examples. Among such trophies, illustrated in this chapter, are those of the New York Ontario and Western, the Philadelphia and Reading, the Pere Marquette, the Erie, and even the New York Central, now merged into the Penn Central System.

Two modern lanterns. The kerosene type is marked CVRY for Central Vermont Railway, and the battery-powered model is marked SPCO for the Southern Pacific Company.

Other pieces of railroad lighting equipment that have interest for the collector are the signal lamps used on switches to indicate whether a switch had been thrown in the proper direction, the lanterns that hung on the rear of freight trains' cabooses, locomotive headlamps, and interior lighting devices from passenger and train-men's cars. Many of these older lamps have been cleaned, repainted, and electrified for regular house current and used as decorative accessories in restaurants, clubs, and the homes of railroad buffs.

A very popular category of railroad hardware is switch keys and

Lantern to be hung on rear of caboose.

Switch-stand lamp finished in yellow paint without targets.

Railroad switch-stand lamp with red and green lenses and flared reflectors called "targets."

Some railroads required employees to surrender a lamp check before issuing them a lantern.

Lantern made to be attached to wall of caboose.

Railroads have always used large
numbers of locks and keys to protect
switches and safeguard other railroad
property. Because most railroad men
were issued and retained the keys
required for their jobs, there are a great
many still available. Collectors try to
acquire different types of locks and as
many keys marked with a railroad's
initials as they can.

Headlamp from Louisiana and Midland Railroad locomotive built by Baldwin in 1913.

locks. These can be collected in great number and variety, and a sizable collection will represent railroad lines from across the continent. Often these items can be bought from the estates of men who once worked for the railroads, since they, more than any other single item of railroading hardware, seem to have been produced in abundance. Because they were necessary to the safety of running the trains, there was little danger of a railroad running out of them, and the surplus, probably thought to have been lost, often ended up in the homes of the men who used them.

It has been the custom for railroads to protect with heavy padlocks the switches along a right-of-way and the shanties containing railroad property. The keys for these locks were issued to all railroad personnel who needed them, and they were kept by the men the whole time they worked for that particular railroad. When a man was fired, quit, or retired, he was expected to turn in his keys. Apparently not all did so, as the large number of switch keys now found in private collections, museums, and dealers' stocks attests.

Aside from a relatively few examples in steel, most keys were made of brass with the initials of the railroad that owned them stamped on the metal. The locks worked by these keys, usually also of brass, were very substantially made to withstand years of hard usage and exposure to extremes of weather.

In the United States the largest supplier to the railroads of locks and keys has been the Adams and Westlake Company of Chicago, which has been making locks and keys for about one hundred years. Other companies that manufactured railroad locks and keys are the Eagle Lock Company, Slaymaker, J. H. Climax, Fraim, J. L. Howard, and W. Bohannan.

Collectors who specialize in switch keys and locks strive to gather as many as possible that represent a variety of railways with as large a geographic distribution as they can find. Since most of the switch keys and matching locks were impressed with the initials of the railroad for which they were made, it is necessary for collectors to have a rather thorough knowledge of the names of all the American railroads, both popular and obscure, in order to identify the specimens they are apt to find. As with most items in railroadiana, the more obscure the railroad, the more valuable the lock and key.

All marked items of hardware used both in the train and the depot are items of interest to certain collectors. Among the identifiable railroad items for which collectors search today are water cans, oil cans, and any items having to do with railroad communications.

This latter group would include telegraphy equipment going back to the mid-nineteenth century. That was the time when the railroad telegrapher would click out train information on his Morse key to the agent in the next depot along the line. A photo in this chapter shows how the operators used an empty tobacco tin to amplify the sound of the incoming signal. This was done so that they could perform other duties, instead of sitting hunched over the apparatus waiting to record messages.

The later high-speed telegraph equipment eventually gave way to the telephone, which was faster, simpler, and did not require trained operators.

Early railroad telegrapher's outfit. Receiver was mounted in a wooden cubby-hole and operator placed empty tobacco tin behind receiver as an aid in improving amplification of signal.

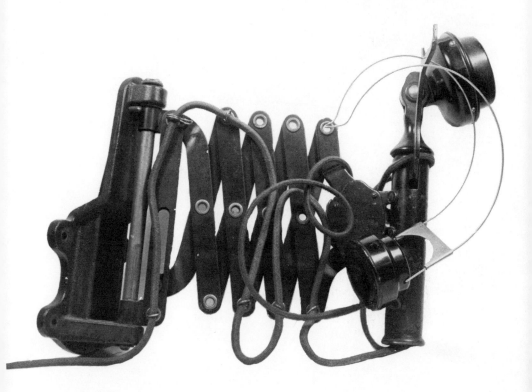

Wall-mounted railroad telephone with scissors-type extension. Earphone that clamped over the head left both hands free.

Compressed-air train whistle from New York City subway train.

High-speed railroad telegraphy transmitting set.

Motorman's throttle from New York City BMT (Brooklyn-Manhattan Transit) subway train.

Water container for railroad
work crew. Marked
N.Y. N.H.& H.R.R.

4

Annual Passes, Baggage Checks, Tickets, and Ticket Machinery

I N 1 9 2 8 a young man from Connecticut inherited an estate from his father and among the various business enterprises of which he found himself in charge was a railroad about six miles long. It was family-built and family-owned, and it had originally been used to haul mica from a mine that had since been exhausted. The railroad was run only to carry coal to a wire mill and to accommodate a few passengers who lived along the line and who had become used to this convenient mode of travel.

The young man became president of this short railroad, and he soon realized his position offered some advantages that might outweigh the headaches. He attended a convention of railroad presidents held that year in Atlantic City, and although he was not able to arrive in a private car, as did the presidents of larger railways, he was able to travel on other railroads free.

While at the convention, the young man was introduced to another railroad president whose line was of much greater size and importance. "I would like to present you with an annual pass to my railroad," he said to the president of the Pennsylvania Railroad.

The older man looked at the pass and said, "I never heard of your railroad." Courtesy demanded that he return the favor by issuing the young president an annual pass to his railroad. "It can't be very big or important."

"No, it's a short railroad," said the young man. "I can understand why you might not have heard of it."

"Well," said the older man. "Mine is a long railroad, and it covers many miles."

"Yes, I know," said the younger man, "but mine is just as wide as yours." He was issued an annual pass on the Pennsylvania, and was able that year to do a fair amount of traveling.

The small pasteboard cards that were issued to allow free travel on the nation's railroads in the latter part of the nineteenth century and the early days of this century are more than simple artifacts that represent a nostalgic period in the history of railroading. Annual passes are collected for many reasons, not the least of which is that today they tell a story of all that was inequitable in the establishment of rates and charges during railroading's golden era. They were badges of influence and importance for those who carried them, and more often than not they represented a form of bribery by the railroad executives to those citizens who might be of some influence in giving the railroads what they asked for in the way of advantages.

Annual passes were freely issued to legislators, judges, and especially to members of the press, who would then be expected to react favorably in any dispute between the railroads and the general public. By giving out these free tickets to everywhere, the moguls of railroading were thus able to establish their own invisible government that would continue to make it possible for them to make fortunes by using what were really public highways.

Judging by the number of annual passes that still exist, it is evident that many thousands of privileged people rode the trains free while others were overcharged to make up the difference. Merchants and manufacturers who depended upon the railroads for portage of their goods felt that they were overcharged to make up the losses caused by giving so many others a free ride.

Another large body of travelers who seldom paid fare on the railroad consisted of railroad executives. Their families were often included in this courtesy. There are many annual passes to be found today that designate the railroad position held by the pass recipient,

Of the railroads represented by these eight annual passes only the Chicago,
Burlington and Quincy is still in existence.

Passes issued from 1867 to 1905 by six railroads operating in Pennsylvania. None of these companies is still in business.

Passes issued by the small railroads that served the mining industry in Colorado are highly desirable collector's items.

and frequently "and wife and children" has been added to the designee's name on the pass. Other family members also seemed to have little difficulty in riding the rails free. "Father and Mother of" many railroad executives were also issued free passes. As with the story of the young president of the short railroad, it was considered a courtesy for railroad men of influence to exchange annual passes with the executives of other lines.

It is doubtful if anyone in the higher management of railroading ever paid his way on a train. Passes were issued rather indiscriminately to any person who might be a friend of management and could possibly be in a position of influence.

Because of their historical importance as well as their beauty, annual passes are a very popular area in the vast field of railroadiana. Collectors search for passes signed by the moguls of railroading in the last quarter of the nineteenth century. The famous or infamous names connected with railroad fortunes are especially in demand. Annual passes signed by a Vanderbilt, Jay Gould, James Hill, and other familiar names are high on every collector's list. Many of the early passes were engraved as carefully as stock certificates or paper money, and often the engravings are on colorful paper. Some cards are illustrated with steam engines or depots, and there are hundreds of passes that represent free rides on railroads that have merged or are now defunct.

All annual passes are dated, and the earliest ones are especially desirable to today's collectors. The small cardboard cards are colorful and make handsome displays when grouped and framed together.

Especially favored personages, such as the President of the United States or the retiring chairman of the board of a major railroad, were occasionally issued lifetime passes engraved on silver. There are even reports that some passes were engraved on gold. These, of course, are extremely rare, and very few of them are known to remain in the hands of private collectors. Most of these intrinsically valuable annual or lifetime passes have long found their way into museums.

It was unusual in the late nineteenth century for any traveler going more than a short distance to travel light, and one writer, discussing railway passenger service at that time, said that the original allowance of fourteen pounds of luggage was "found to be

These two passes are of special interest as the Erie pass bears the signature of Jay Gould, and the New York Central and Hudson River pass was signed by a Vanderbilt.

Brass baggage checks used by railroads to route passenger's luggage and also as claim checks.

increased to four hundred when ladies start for fashionable summer-resorts." At that time few of the railroads charged for excess baggage.

The baggage-check system is one that was implemented out of necessity. Originally passengers were allowed to identify and carry away their own baggage at their point of destination. This led to much confusion, frequent losses, and heavy claims upon the railroad companies as a consequence. It is of interest that many of today's airlines have not improved on this method for claiming baggage and some of the same problems exist in their handling of luggage that prevailed in the early days of railroading.

The railroads went about solving their problem in a logical fashion. As General Horace Porter, vice-president of the Pullman Palace-Car Company, wrote in 1888: "Necessity, as usual, gave birth to invention, and the difficulty was at last solved by the introduction of the system known as 'checking.'" Metal disks bearing a number and designating on its face the destination of the baggage was attached to each article and a duplicate was given to the owner. The complication of arranging baggage for through trips over many connecting roads was soon solved, and the check system became so advanced that the express or transfer company would pick up the baggage at a passenger's home, check it through, and see that the baggage was delivered at any given address.

The use of baggage checks solved a great problem for the railroads, and the cost was offset by there being fewer articles lost and thus fewer claims against the railroads. Interestingly the use of baggage checks seems to have been an American innovation and one that was not generally adopted by European railways.

Augusta, Georgia,
to
Harrisburg, Pa.

via

GEORGIA R. R.
WESTERN & ATLANTIC RR
E. TENN., VA. & GEORGIA R.R.
NORFOLK & WESTERN R.R.
SHENNANDOAH VALLEY RR
and
CUMBERLAND VALLEY R. R.

Circa 1880

Check accompanying baggage from Augusta, Ga., to Harrisburg, Pa. included routing over the line's six railroads.

Rare baggage check from Alaskan railroad.

81

This use of baggage tokens has provided today's collectors of railroadiana with another interesting group of objects associated with early train travel. Those tokens dating from the nineteenth century are somewhat difficult to find, but they do exist in many collections. All checks are marked with the name of the railroad on which they were used.

Remote or defunct or merged railroads have contributed the most important collector's items in this category, and the metal tokens now conjure up in the minds of those who own them days of the great Saratoga trunks and a time in the history of travel when an indication of a traveler's affluence was measured by the number of pieces of luggage that went along on any overnight trip.

Old railway passenger tickets evoke a great deal of nostalgia as many were issued by railroads no longer in business. These are often displayed framed in groups.

Tickets and ticket punches are yet another class of railroadiana that has a large number of fans. Although collectors search for the earliest tickets they can find, the ones that are in greatest demand are the colorfully printed tickets that were used after 1880.

Both punched and unpunched tickets seem to be of equal interest to collectors, since most of the tickets that have survived represent railroads that haven't. Every ticket punch used on a line was different, and all were easily recognizable to every conductor on a line. An almost infinite amount of punch shapes could be devised for the longer passenger routes, so that a conductor could tell just how far a passenger had traveled on his ticket. Tickets were printed in a great variety of colors on heavy pasteboard, and many have survived from the last century in good condition.

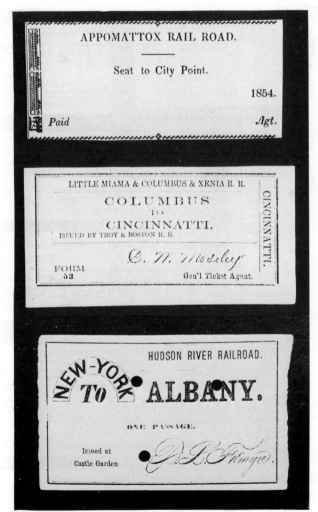

Three very early railway tickets. The top ticket, dated 1854, bears a very interesting drawing of an old steam engine and passenger cars.

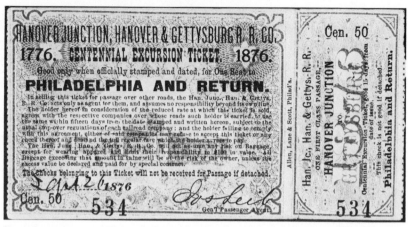

Excursion ticket from Hanover, Pennsylvania, to 1876 Centennial Exposition in Philadelphia.

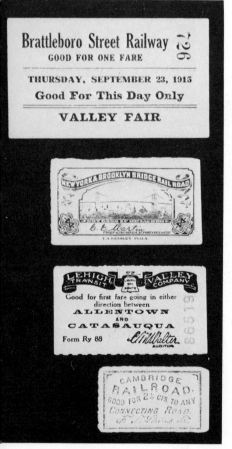

Daily commuter's ticket dated 1875 for rides on the Pennsylvania Railroad between Linden, N.J., and New York City.

Four early trolley or interurban railway tickets.

Cosmo No. 4 ticket stamping and cutting machine.

Brass ticket stamping dies from four stations on the Illinois Central Railroad. Date was inserted in the openings in each die.

Freight and ticket hand stamps from six
different railroads. Photograph is reversed so
that engraving can be read.

Hill's Model A "Centennial" ticket validating machine, c. 1876.

Conductor's hand punch with box in which it was originally sold.

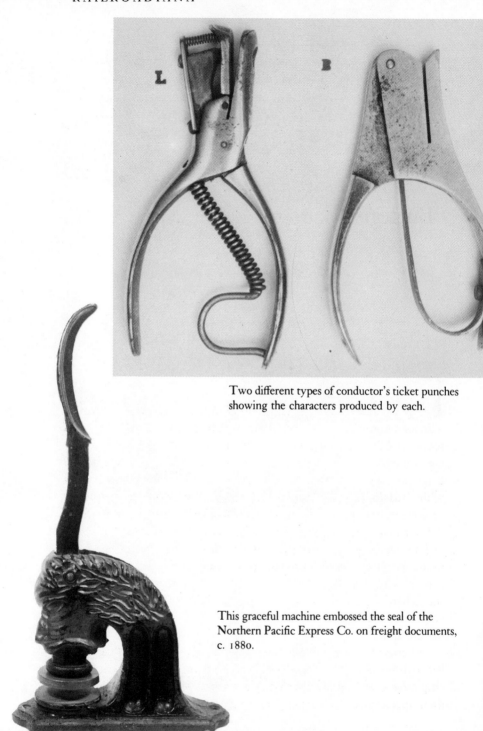

Two different types of conductor's ticket punches showing the characters produced by each.

This graceful machine embossed the seal of the Northern Pacific Express Co. on freight documents, c. 1880.

5

Railroad Uniform Items—
Buttons, Badges, Patches, and Caps

I T W A S not until late in the nineteenth century that railroad management dressed its employees in clothing that made them easily recognizable to passengers. In 1888 the associate editor of *Railroad Gazette* wrote, "The wearing of uniforms has been introduced from England and is, in the main, a good feature, though some roads, whose discipline is otherwise quite good, allow their men to appear in slovenly and even ragged clothes." Evidently, the use of uniforms did not make all employees happy since this same author also stated, "[The wearing of uniforms] affects the men's self-respect and influences their usefulness in other ways. The frugal brakeman cannot wear his blue suit on Sunday or a-visiting, and his Sunday suit when old cannot be used up by weekday wear, so he naturally concludes that his employer is guilty of a little undue severity toward him."

When railroad employees were uniformed, certain problems that had existed before were solved. The position held by a uniformed employee could be ascertained at a glance; the men were neater in their appearance; and passengers were less reluctant to give up their tickets to men whose clothing designated that they were only fulfilling their duties.

A story was told in the late nineteenth century that points out the necessity for uniforms, especially for conductors. A United States senator-elect from the Far West, who had traveled east by sea, had never before been on or perhaps never even seen a train until his return journey. He bought a ticket to Cincinnati, entered a passenger car, and took a seat near the door. The conductor, in ordinary clothing, came up to him and reached out his hand to the senator. When the senator asked him what he wanted, the conductor said, "I want your ticket."

"Don't you think I've got sense enough to know that if I parted with my ticket right at the start, I wouldn't have anything to show for my money during the rest of the way? No, sir, I'm going to hold on to this till I get to the end of the trip," the senator said.

Assurance from the conductor that he didn't want to keep the ticket but only wanted to look at it failed to convince the senator that he should comply. The conductor lost his patience and tore the ticket out of the passenger's hand. A fight ensued, and the senator landed a blow on the conductor's eye. It was some time before the rest of the passengers could convince him that the conductor had every right to inspect the ticket. If the conductor had been dressed in a uniform, the senator would never have questioned his authority.

All remnants of old uniforms worn by railroad personnel are considered collectible today. Caps are especially in demand, and those that once belonged to conductors, brakemen, passenger agents, and other agents of the railroad are highly prized. Usually the position as well as the railroad line's name or initials are embroidered on the cap.

Cap badges that adorned the caps of uniformed railroad employees are another popular category of collectible. Those that represent defunct or merged railroads are particularly valued; they are scarce and somewhat expensive today. Collections of cap badges are usually mounted on boards and sometimes framed to make handsome and nostalgic displays.

The badges were made from a variety of metals, but most are brass and nickel plated. Some of them have been enameled and are very colorful. There is an almost endless variety of shapes to be found in cap badges from curved or scalloped edges to straight

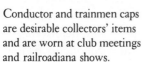

Conductor and trainmen caps are desirable collectors' items and are worn at club meetings and railroadiana shows.

Railroad employees' cap badges.

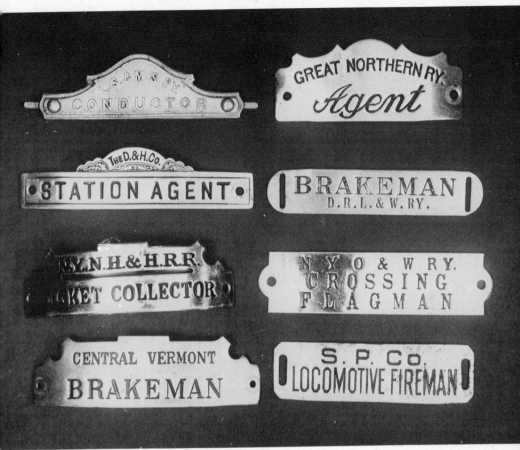

Railroad employees' cap badges.

rectangular badges. Cap badges are still in somewhat ample supply, except for those that represent short-run lines. Most of the rarities are already in important private collections, and new collectors will have to wait until the day arrives that these rarities are auctioned or sold privately. For those collectors who are not determined to have badges that represent the railroad lines that only operated for a short period of time, a rather extensive collection can still be gathered.

All railroad enthusiasts like to own at least one cap complete with badge and buttons. Many collectors do not stop at one cap and strive to find caps that represent all phases of railroad occupations on a particular line or more than one conductor's cap from a variety of lines or name trains. At any gathering of railroadiana collectors

Conductors' cap badges from trolley systems and railroads.

Motormen's cap and uniform badges from trolley and interurban railway lines.

many dealers and members will be found wearing their favorite caps, and more than one model-railroad enthusiast dons his engineer's cap before turning on the switch. It is rare when complete turn-of-the-century uniforms become available for sale, and they are quickly purchased when they can be found in good condition.

Some collectors are content to gather a variety of cloth patches that have been salvaged from old railroad uniforms and caps. These embroidered patches designate the various positions for which uniforms were issued and the initials or names of the railroads that issued them. The embroidered lettering on a uniform or cap would tell the passenger that a man was in charge of "lost articles," "baggage," or "information." The patches, usually machine-embroidered in gold thread, are frequently sewn onto new garments worn by railroadiana collectors.

Brass job-description insignia designed to be attached to employees' caps.

Uniform buttons are another very popular specialty among collectors. While there are thousands of button collectors, it takes people of very specialized interests to limit such a collection to buttons made specifically for railroad employees' uniforms. Buttons were made in special sizes for coat fronts, cuffs, and sometimes for the sides of caps. The many categories of railroad buttons include those worn by employees of trolley, horsecar, monorail, elevated, subway, cable-car lines and interurban companies. Obviously, there can be a huge selection in this category of railroadiana. Many button collectors do not limit themselves to the railways of America, but search for buttons that represent the railways of the world.

Most American railroad uniform buttons were made of copper alloys and are brass-colored. During the period from 1888 to around 1915, aluminum buttons were made in the United States. Some Japanese buttons were made of wood, and later buttons, especially those of Canada, were made of plastic. British World War I and II buttons were made of hard rubber or composition, and there are glass and plastic buttons being used for railroad uniforms in parts of Europe today.

The brass buttons used in the United States were made by the same methods as military uniform buttons and the same two companies, the Waterbury Company and the Scovill Manufacturing Company of Waterbury, Connecticut, have a century-old tradition of producing buttons for both the military and the railroads. These companies are the only manufacturers left that still produce dies from which the metal uniform buttons are stamped. A company that made railroad buttons in the past is the D. Evans Company of Attleboro, Massachusetts. Many of the backs of railroad uniform buttons are marked only with the name of the tailor who ordered the buttons for the uniforms he made.

Since the idea of dressing railroad employees in uniforms originated in England, many of the earliest American uniforms were ordered from that country, and brass buttons can be found that have the mark of a British maker and the insignia of an American railroad.

The fronts of the buttons are what appeal to most collectors of railroadiana, who are less interested in the manufacturer than they are in railroad history. On the buttons can be found the many insignia of the early railroads, and collectors often specialize in those

Railroad employees' uniform buttons from thirty-one different railroads.

Railroad employees' pins in recognition of years of service and promoting safety.

Enameled brass lapel buttons.

buttons that represent a specific line in which they are interested. A "Long Island" collector, for instance, might search through boxes of old buttons for one that will round out his collection of artifacts from just that one line.

There is no shortage of railroad uniform buttons, but certainly the buttons that represent merged or defunct railroads, trolley lines, and so forth, are difficult to find. The collector who specializes in railroad buttons must compete with many other button collectors who have no particular interest in the railroads but search for all kinds of historical buttons. In addition, those collectors who are searching for special buttons often have a lengthy and frustrating job of hunting through boxes of buttons until the elusive button from a special railroad is found.

Railroad-police badges from Atlantic Coast Line, Long Island, Chesapeake and Ohio, Lehigh Valley, and Boston and Maine railroads.

6

Dining-Car Collectibles—
China, Silver, Linens, and Menus

D INNER in the diner" used to be the highlight of any long train trip, and there are collectors today who look for any of the objects that remind them of that aspect of what seems from this distance to have been a gracious way to travel. All silver serving pieces, flatware, dishes, linens, and other dining-car equipment are collected today. Just about everything used for the serving of meals on the great trains was monogrammed, certainly for the advertising value and probably to keep passengers from removing these articles and taking them home as souvenirs of a once-in-a-lifetime trip.

The earliest passenger trains had no provision for serving meals, and passengers brought their own food or bought it at railroad stations along the route when a five- or ten-minute wait would give them the opportunity to rush in and grab a fast and often unappetizing sandwich. The passengers were a captive market for the railroads, and the station restaurants were undoubtedly a profitable enterprise, but after the introduction of the parlor car and especially of Mr. Pullman's sleeping car, it became obvious that there was little point in stopping at a station for meals. As General Porter, vice-president of the Pullman Palace-Car Company, wrote in 1893, "Why should a train stop at a station for meals any more than a steamboat tie up to a wharf for the same purpose?" The

Oval plate supplied by the Pullman Company and made by Syracuse China.

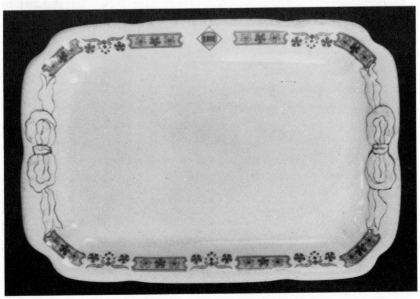

Change plate made for Erie Railroad.

Serving dish, Maine Central Railroad.

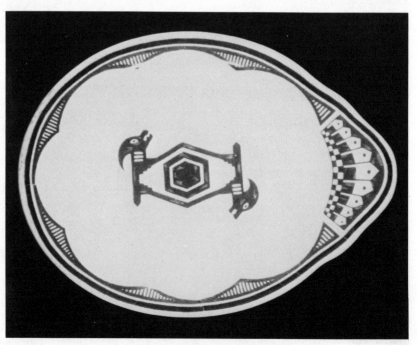

Dish with Southwest Indian motif used by the Santa Fe.

Pullman Company introduced the hotel-car in 1867. This was a sleeping car with a kitchen and pantries at one end, and portable tables that could be placed between the seats of each section and upon which meals could be served.

The first hotel-car was named the President and was put into service on the Great Western Railway of Canada in 1867. It was not long before other popular lines added a similar service. The dining car was a natural follow-up to the hotel-car. This was, of course, a complete restaurant which had the kitchen and pantries at one end of the railway car and tables and chairs in the remainder of the space. The first dining car was named the Delmonico, and was put into service on the Chicago and Alton Railroad in 1868.

Dining cars were run as first-class restaurants with lengthy menus and elegant silver, glassware, and china. Certain lines became known for specialties in their cuisines, and passengers would be offered regional food as they passed through the states for which it

Inca Ware oval plate, Western Pacific Railroad, marked Shenango China/Newcastle, Pa.

Saucer, Union Pacific Railroad, made by Shenango China.

Chicago, Rock Island and
Pacific Railroad dinner
plate promoting its
"Rocket" streamlined
passenger trains.

Postcard printed for Northern Pacific Railway shows interior of one of the line's dining cars of 1910 vintage.

Interior of dining car on Pennsylvania's Broadway Limited. This promotional folder, printed in the 1930's, shows Art Deco decor.

Individual bean pot from New York, New Haven and
Hartford Railroad.

was noted. The Northern Pacific, which ran through the state of
Idaho, was famous for its huge baked potatoes. Great meals with
endless courses and fine wines were available to make travelers
forget that the cars were extremely hot and stuffy in warm weather
and one's feet often numb with cold in northern climates. Bostoni-
ans using the New York, New Haven and Hartford Railroad could
feel at home when their baked beans were served in individual bean
pots monogrammed with the name of the railroad.

   Although eastern travelers who could afford them had the
convenience and luxury of the Pullman hotel-cars during the 1870's,
western travelers were still at the mercy of the depot lunch counters.
Since the counters were often primitive and dirty, it was obvious
that better facilities were necessary or at least desirable. Frederick
Henry Harvey, with a background of restaurateur, railway mail

Northern Pacific souvenir item promoting railway's slogan of the line with the
"great big baked potato."

clerk and freight agent, convinced the management of the Atchison, Topeka and Santa Fe Railroad to open the first decent depot restaurant under his management in the railroad's Topeka, Kansas, depot and office building in 1876. Harvey's next venture was in Florence, Kansas, where he started a restaurant and hotel for railroad travelers, and an agreement was then made that Harvey would open additional facilities for the Santa Fe and that the railroad would furnish premises and equipment while Harvey provided the food and service. By 1900 Harvey and the railroad were partners in fifteen hotels, forty-seven restaurants, and thirty dining cars. Harvey's accommodations were clean and neat, and certainly more honest and attractive than the depot lunch counters had been. In addition, Harvey helped to settle the West by hiring young girls to serve as waitresses in his restaurants, and many of these disciplined and attractive women stayed on in the West to marry railroad employees or travelers whom they met while working. All Harvey House memorabilia, including photographs of the attractive uniformed Harvey girls, are in demand today.

For collectors of dining-car china, there is a great variety of patterns and shapes to be found. Most of the china made especially for railroad dining cars is heavy and serviceable. There is evidence that in the earliest days of the dining car stock china patterns were used, and these were undoubtedly made of the sort of porcelain found in fine restaurants of the period. Little of it has survived, and since it was not monogrammed, the little that has is difficult to identify. Most of the railroad china that can be collected today is of a later date and was undoubtedly made to last. Special patterns were designed for each train or railway, and certain patterns have become scarce and very desirable to today's collector. One allover pattern derived from earlier Staffordshire blue-and-white dishes made with historical motifs or scenic designs was produced to order for the Baltimore and Ohio Railroad for its centennial in 1927. Twenty-one shapes and patterns make up this set of dishes that has a border of the famous B & O locomotives and the dates when they were built. The center designs are from engravings of scenes found along the main route of the railway. The original set of B & O dishes was made by the Scammell China Company of Trenton, New Jersey, and the first issue is marked with a shield on the back describing the occasion of the plate design. Later issues of the same pattern were marked "Lamberton China."

Blue and white commemorative ware made for the Baltimore and Ohio Railroad.

Almost all railroad china produced for American railroads was supplied by American manufacturers. The Lamberton Works, owned by D. William Scammell, probably made more railroad china than anyone else in the first three decades of this century. Other railroad china was supplied by manufacturers in Syracuse and Rochester, New York. Before the turn of the century most china made for domestic use was imported from England, France, and China, and there is little doubt that the orders and reorders for plates for dining cars helped to establish the American ceramic industry.

There are several reasons why it was important that the railroads use American manufacturers for their china. For one thing, railroad purchasing agents could work closely with the ceramic designers to establish patterns that were suitable to each train or railway. In addition, the railroads had to be able to reorder huge quantities of dishes in the same patterns for replacements. It is obvious, that even with the heavy semiporcelain plates, there would be considerable breakage on dining cars. No chipped or cracked crockery could be

Prairie Mountain Wildflowers pattern, made for Southern Pacific Lines by Onandaga Pottery Co., Syracuse, New York.

Illinois Central Railroad plate in the Coral pattern, made by Syracuse China.

Great Northern Railway saucer with scenic design, made by Syracuse China.

Electroliner plate, Chicago, North Shore and Milwaukee Railroad. Train was in service for short period in early 1940's.

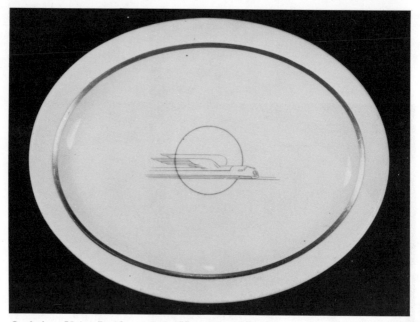

Oval plate, Union Pacific, made by Homer Laughlin Co.

Plate dated 1921 commemorating reunion of employees of the Lake Shore and Michigan Southern Railway, which was absorbed by the New York Central in the late nineteenth century.

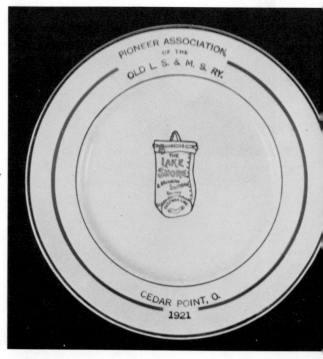

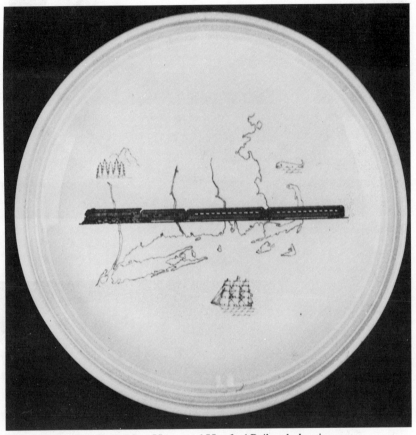

Dinner plate, New York, New Haven and Hartford Railroad, showing steam locomotive traversing part of New England served by the railroad.

Three styles of New York Central cups and saucers.

Cup and saucer and creamer, Wabash Railroad, now part of the Penn Central System.

Compote and dish,
Denver and Rio Grande
Western Railroad, made
by Syracuse China.

used, and constant reorders were necessary to keep each dining car on a line well equipped.

It is still possible with certain designs to put together an entire service of one pattern of dining-car china. Many collectors patiently do so, while others strive to collect at least one piece from every known available pattern of dining-car china. A few collectors specialize in a single shape, such as a dinner plate or demitasse cup and saucer. The dining-car dinner plates were frequently oval in shape, since in this way they would take up less table space. Other collectors specialize in the Art Deco patterns of some of the early

Creamer, Baltimore and Ohio Railroad.

Individual cream servers. Pennsylvania Railroad piece marked Scammell's/Lamberton China/John Wanamaker.

Trivet made by Buffalo China Co. Serving dish made by Hall Bros. China. Both used on New York, New Haven and Hartford Railroad.

Matchholder, the New England Steamship Company, which was owned by the New York, New Haven and Hartford Railroad, made by Buffalo China Co.

Egg cup, New York Central, DeWitt Clinton pattern. Soup cup, Norfolk & Western Railway.

streamliners. All collectors search for patterns that were specially designed and exclusive only to the railways or trains for which they were made. Most plates have a monogram either on the front as part of the pattern or on the back with the name of the railroad for which they were made. A few plates have a design of the train itself, and these are in high demand among collectors who search for anything with a picture of a train on it.

It is doubtful if any of the trains used sterling silver flatware, but there was a great variety of plated forks, knives, and spoons all especially designed and monogrammed for each individual line. Some have the railroad logo on the front, while others have the train or railway name on the reverse. Most of the available railroad silver is representative of the streamliners of the thirties, and much of it is

Left to right, sugar spoon, Southern Railway; teaspoons, Rock Island, Atlantic Coast Line; ice tea spoons, Baltimore and Ohio, Erie.

Dinner knives, *left to right*, Norfolk and Western, Southern Railway, Wabash, New York Central.

Dinner forks, *left to right*, Pennsylvania Railroad, Canadian National Railway, Bangor and Aroostook, Baltimore and Ohio.

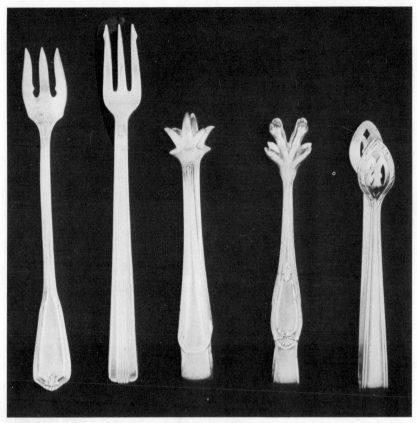

Left to right, pickle forks, New York Central; sugar tongs, New York, New Haven and Hartford Railroad.

in Art Deco designs that suggest the streamlined motifs that were prevalent in the decorative arts of the period. Frequently the serving pieces in railroad silver flatware are more elegant in design. Again American silversmiths were the manufacturers of railroad silver, and Gorham of Providence, Rhode Island, and Reed and Barton of Taunton, Massachusetts, were the companies that seemed to produce most of the railroad flatware and hollow ware.

There is a great variety of hollow serving pieces that attest to the elegance of service on railway dining cars in the first half of this century. Individual coffee-pots, stemmed dessert dishes, bonbon

121

Teapot and sugar bowl, New York, New Haven and Hartford Railroad.

Creamer, Chicago, Milwaukee, St. Paul and Pacific Railroad, Hiawatha pattern; coffeepot, Atchison, Topeka and Santa Fe Railway.

Tea service, New York, New Haven and Hartford Railroad.

Coffeepot, New York Central Railroad.

Toothpick holder, Baltimore and Ohio Railroad; finger bowl, Southern Pacific; tabasco holder, New York, New Haven and Hartford Railroad.

Gravy boat, Seaboard Air Line.

Ice-cream dishes, New York, New Haven and Hartford Railroad.

dishes, water carafes, and even tabasco-sauce holders make it easy to picture the days when the railroad passenger was coddled and catered to. Because the serving pieces were required to be sturdier than china, most of them were made of metal. Many of the silver serving pieces were heavily monogrammed; also, most are of simple and classic patterns, while a few can be found in the streamlined designs of Art Deco.

Of all dining-car appurtenances that survive, the old menus are perhaps the most interesting. They show that a meal could go on for many courses and that wines were available at all three meals, including breakfast. Courses were almost endless, and on some lines fresh brook trout and fresh pineapple and other fruits that were considered exotic at the time were regular parts of the bill of fare. Perhaps one of the reasons that these elaborate old menus are in such demand today is the nostalgia one feels upon reading that the best in

Menu holder, New York Central Railroad.

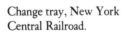

Change tray, New York
Central Railroad.

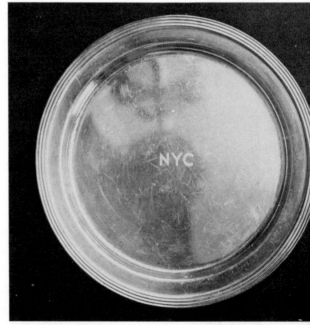

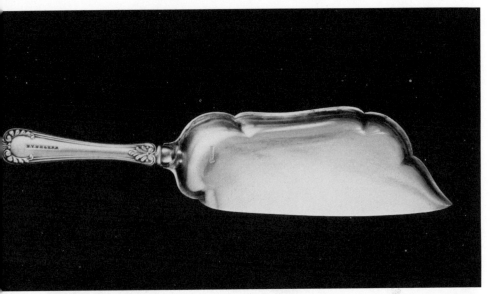

Crumber, New York, New Haven and Hartford Railroad.

Wine cooler, Shore Line Division of New York, New Haven and Hartford Railroad.

Thermos bottles for
water, Pullman Company.

Linens, such as head-rest covers, tablecloths, and napkins, even sheets and pillow
cases, with the railroad's name embroidered on them have become a collectible
category.

No Pullman car was complete without its spittoon, and the jug of deodorizer was used to clean up after those who missed.

the HIAWATHA

Thunderbird design from Menomoni tribe woven bag, common in Western Great Lakes area.

THE MILWAUKEE ROAD

Chicago, Milwaukee, St. Paul and Pacific's menu for its Chicago-Seattle Hiawatha streamliner passenger trains. Thunderbird motif was adapted from Menomoni Indians of the western Great Lakes area.

129

dining-car service and food was available for a small fraction of what the worst restaurant meal would cost today. If anything makes one long for "the good old days," a menu from 1906 that lists a seven-course luncheon for $1.00 or a Christmas menu where "choice stand of beef, drip gravy" is only $.50 can make one wish for a time machine. In addition to the mouth-watering reading matter within, great care was taken by the railways to offer menus with attractively designed covers. Unlike the china and silver, the menus were meant to be stuffed into a traveler's suitcase and taken home as a souvenir and advertisement of the elegant dining-car service available on that railroad.

Northern Pacific's 1910 Christmas dinner menu. The most expensive item is tenderloin or sirloin steak at 80¢.

Christmas

Oysters	BLUE POINTS ON THE SHELL, 25 OYSTER COCKTAIL, M. & O. SAUCE, 25 CREAM STEW, 40 MILK STEW, 30 FRIED BON SECOUR OYSTERS, 30
Soups	MOCK TURTLE, 25 CHICKEN GUMBO, 25 TOMATO, 25 CLAM CHOWDER, 25 MULLIGATAWNY, 25
Relishes	QUEEN OLIVES, 15 SWEET GHERKINS, 10 CORN RELISH, 15 STUFFED OLIVES, 15 SLICED TOMATOES, 20 NEW CELERY, 15
Fish	BAKED RED SNAPPER, CREOLE SAUCE, 50 SPANISH MACKEREL, 50
Roast	CHOICE PRIME STAND OF BEEF, DRIP GRAVY, 50 ROAST YOUNG TURKEY, OYSTER DRESSING, 50 STUFFED QUAIL WITH BACON, 60
Grilled	TENDERLOIN STEAK, 80 SIRLOIN STEAK, 80 BROILED SPRING CHICKEN, CORN FRITTER, 50 MUTTON CHOPS, ON TOAST, 50
Cold Dishes	CAVIAR ON TOAST, 40 BOSTON BAKED BEANS, 25 IMPORTED SARDINES, 35 OX TONGUE, 35
Salad	LETTUCE AND TOMATO, 25
Potatoes and Vegetables	FRIED SWEET POTATOES, 15 MASHED OR BOILED POTATOES, 10 SARATOGA CHIPS, 10 ASPARAGUS ON TOAST, 20 FRENCH PEAS, 20 SPICED MUSHROOMS, 20 STEWED TOMATOES, 15 LIMA BEANS, 15 STEWED CORN, 15

Canadian Pacific
DINING CAR SERVICE

The Canadian Pacific Railway issued a colorful assortment of menu covers in the 1950's showing typical Canadian scenes.

One of a series of menu covers drawn for the Illinois Central Railroad by artist Phil Austin depicting scenes along the I.C. route.

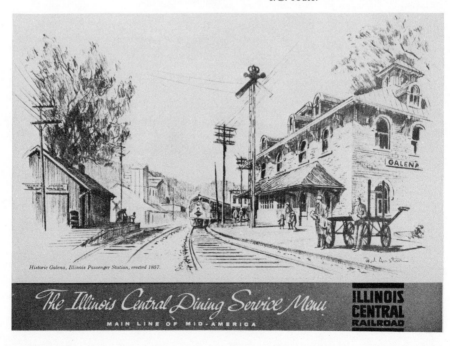

Historic Galena, Illinois Passenger Station, erected 1857.

The Illinois Central Dining Service Menu

MAIN LINE OF MID-AMERICA

ILLINOIS CENTRAL RAILROAD

The Pennsylvania Railroad's Broadway Limited carried Art Deco dining-car design onto this menu cover with New York City night scene.

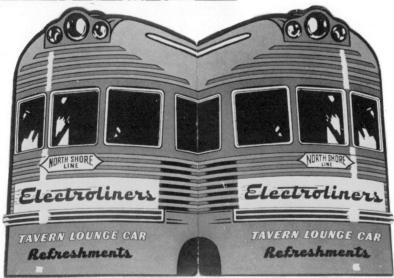

Menu cover die-cut and printed to simulate appearance of Electroliner trains, which ran between Chicago and Milwaukee in early 1940's.

Back cover of 1879 Hannibal and St. Joseph Rail Road timetable, showing cutaway view of early reclining-seat passenger car.

Hannibal and St. Joseph Rail Road timetable unfolds to reveal map of the railroad's route and a drawing of a steam locomotive of the period hauling a mail car and three passenger cars.

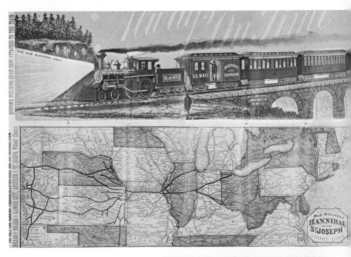

LEFT: Unfolded cover of October 1903 Colorado Midland Railway timetable. The timetables of this short-lived narrow-gauge line are prized by collectors both for their rarity and beauty. RIGHT: Carolina Clinchfield and Ohio Railway timetables are desirable because of the scenic views reproduced for the benefit of passengers on what was principally a coal-hauling rail line.

Three Kansas City Southern Railway timetables from 1901 and 1903. Timetable at left shows lighthouse at Port Arthur, Texas, the line's southern terminus. The two timetables at the right employ a crow to suggest the road's slogan, "Straight as the Crow Flies."

LEFT: Only known issue of Keokuk and Western Railroad Company timetable incorporating a striking portrait of Keokuk, chief of the Sac and Fox tribes for whom the city of Keokuk, Iowa, was named in 1829. RIGHT: Timetable of defunct California Northwestern Railway has appealing picture of a small boy in a conductor's uniform and scenic views of northern California.

The St. Louis-San Francisco Railway, which does not go to San Francisco, published this timetable which emphasizes the routes it does serve, principally from St. Louis to Oklahoma and Texas.

Picturesque timetable of the Richmond and Danville Railroad which operated in Virginia until it became part of the Southern Railway system. "French Broad Route" refers to the name of a river on the line's western North Carolina division.

Florida Central and Peninsular Railroad timecard dated Feb. 10, 1893. This route later became part of the Atlantic Coast Line. Female figure representing Florida is shown holding a huge orange on which is a map of the road's rail lines.

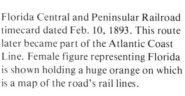

Two trolley timetables that are collectible in that they are printed in color and have illustrations of women on the covers.

Annual pass issued by the Chicago and Alton Railroad for the year 1896. This example shows Father Time as the engineer.

Nineteenth-century menu supplied by the Michigan Central Railroad. Interesting to rail buffs for interior view of lavishly appointed dining car, including dangerous overhead kerosene lighting fixtures.

In the first decade of the twentieth century the Chicago and Northwestern Railway appealed to the gastronome in this series of postcards printed for the line.

One of a series of four calendars issued in 1906 by the Chicago and Alton Railroad with the female figure in each dressed in a different bird costume.

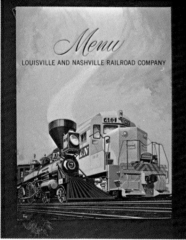

Recent menu cover from the Louisville and Nashville Railroad of interest because of colorful illustration of early steam locomotive and modern diesel.

Southern Pacific calendar for the year 1899, advertising the then fast time of 58 hours from New Orleans to Los Angeles and 75 hours to San Francisco.

One of a series of collectible train illustrations taken from annual calendars published by the New York Central. This 1928 issue shows the Central's crack Twentieth Century Limited with the title "When Winter Comes."

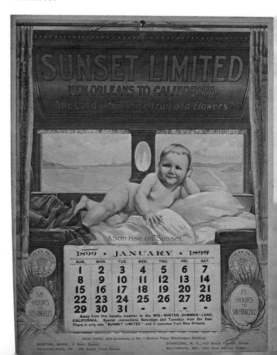

Union Pacific Railroad poster advertising the G.A.R. convention of Union Army veterans of the Civil War held in Denver, Colorado, on July 24, 1883. The copy describes Denver's attractions and the fact that the Union Pacific had four routes into the city.

Appealing nineteenth-century poster, printed for the Chicago, Rock Island and Pacific Railway, showing a young girl with her dog pointing to a map of the route of the Rock Island. In her left hand she holds a sheet of paper listing some of the road's routes. In the background is an illustration of the Union Depot in Chicago.

Perpetual calendar dated 1881 given away by the Continental Fire Insurance Company. This piece is rich in historical associations as it shows a homesteader's cabin, an Indian on horseback, a buffalo stampede, and a train with "New York to San Francisco" lettered on the cars.

Attractive sheet-music cover for a march and two step entitled "Dawn of the Century." Published in 1900, it has contemporary illustrations of telegraph, trolley car, electric generator, internal-combustion engine, telephone, sewing machine, reaper, steam locomotive, and automobile.

The Great Train Robbery was a popular motion picture produced in 1903. This action-filled poster was used to advertise the production.

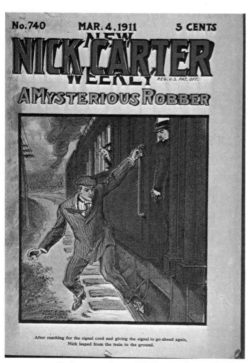

Pulp magazines with illustrations of railroading stories on their covers are a popular collectible. The usual theme involved a young engineer thwarting bandits and rescuing pretty young women.

This poster was published by the Brotherhood of Railroad Trainmen, the largest of the rail unions. Starting in the lower right-hand corner and moving counterclockwise, it depicts a railroad brakeman bidding farewell to his family, a wreck at a collapsed bridge, breaking the news to the widow, the funeral, and the Brotherhood giving a check to the bereaved family.

Among the subjects sought by collectors of railroad-related postcards are those picturing depots and stations. Here is the bizarre pagodalike station in North Conway, New Hampshire.

Good scenic illustrations that include trains make desirable postcards. This 1907 card shows the Rock Island's Rocky Mountain Limited.

This postcard of the Ringling Brothers and Barnum and Bailey Circus unloading their mile-and-a-third-long train of one hundred cars appeals to both circus and rail buffs.

Trolley fans appreciate views such as this postcard of an early twentieth-century open-sided Connecticut trolley car.

Catalogs such as this one issued in 1954 by Lionel had an irresistible appeal for railroad fans of all ages. The old catalogs of all toy-train manufacturers are now avidly sought by collectors.

PENNSYLVANIA RAILROAD

SPECIAL TRAIN

CONVEYING

H. R. H. PRINCE HENRY OF PRUSSIA

PULLMAN DINING CAR "WILLARD"

WINE LIST

CHAMPAGNES
PIPER-HEIDSIECK, SEC, WHITE LABEL   MOËT & CHANDON, BRUT IMPERIAL
G. H. MUMM & CO., EXTRA DRY   POMMERY & GRENO, VIN SEC
POMMERY & GRENO, VIN NATURE   RUINART, BRUT   IRROY, BRUT

GERMAN CHAMPAGNE
RHEINGOLD

VINTAGE CHAMPAGNES
PIPER-HEIDSIECK, BRUT

AMERICAN CHAMPAGNES
COOK'S IMPERIAL, EXTRA DRY   GOLD SEAL, SPECIAL DRY   GREAT WESTERN

CLARETS
ST. JULIEN   PONTET CANET   CHATEAU LAFITTE, 1881   MEDOC

SAUTERNES
GRAVES, DRY   CHATEAU LATOUR BLANCHE, 1886   CHATEAU YQUEM

BURGUNDIES (RED)
BEAUNE, 1889   POMMARD, 1889   CHAMBERTIN, 1881

BURGUNDIES (WHITE)
CHABLIS, 1887

SPARKLING WINE
CABINET MOSELLE

RHINE WINES
DEIDESHEIMER   NIERSTEINER   LIEBFRAUMILCH, 1891

MOSELLE WINES
ZELTINGER   ERDENER TREPPCHEN

CALIFORNIA WINES
LA ROSA, ZINFANDEL, RED   CABINET RIESLING, WHITE
UNFERMENTED GRAPE JUICE, CRYSTAL BRAND

SHERRY WINE
AMONTILLADO PASADO

BRANDIES
OTARD DUPUY & CO., 1878   V. S. O. P. COGNAC, 1840
G. F. CHAMPAGNE COGNAC, 1811

RYE AND BOURBON WHISKIES
WILSON   HUNTER   OLD CROW   PEPPER   EXTRA OLD RYE

SCOTCH AND IRISH WHISKIES
JOHN DEWAR'S SPECIAL   JOHN DEWAR'S EXTRA SPECIAL
KING WILLIAM V. O. P.   JAMESON'S IRISH

ALE
BASS & CO.'S PALE ALE, WHITE LABEL

BEERS (IMPORTED)
PILSNER   CULMBACHER

BEERS (DOMESTIC)
PABST'S BLUE RIBBON   MAERZEN (HEINRICH)   ANHEUSER-BUSCH

MINERAL WATERS
WHITE ROCK   APOLLINARIS   LONDONDERRY LITHIA   POLAND SPARKLING
GERMAN SELTZERS   DELATOUR SODA   SYPHONS   HATHORN
CLUB SODA   GINGER ALE, CANTRELL & COCHRAN
CHAMPAGNE CIDER

Souvenir wine list from special Pennsylvania Railroad train carrying Prince Henry of Prussia on his visit to the United States in 1902.

Appetizers

Hors d'oeuvres	1.25
Hors de combat	100 francs
Low Calorie Juice	.45
High Voltage Juice	.10 per K. W.
Chopped High Livers	1.00
Asparagus Tips	.45
Carrot Tops	20.00
Canned Canard	1.00
Can Can	2.00
Assorted Cold Planters	.75
Plover Eggs	1.25
Golden Goose Eggs	35.00 per ounce

Oysters

On the half shell	.65
with Artificial Pearl	1.65 plus tax
with Cultured Pearl	2.65 plus tax
with Oriental Pearl	3.65 plus tax
with Mother of Pearl	4.65
with Pearl	4.65 plus 15.35 Tip

Soup

Green Turtle	.85
Red Herring	.85
Diamond Back Terrapin with drawn butter	.75
Bareback Taxpayer with drawn blood	.50
Split Pea	.85
Split Infinitives	.85
Split Dixiecrats with Frozen Assets	.20
Boula-Boula	.15

Sea Foods

Fillet of Flounder		1.00
Floundering Filly	New York	20.00
	Southampton	40.00
Imported Jerked Filling		.60
Domestic Soft Warps with Gremlins		.60
Pate of Young Shrimp		1.00
Pinch of Old Shrimp		.50
Backfin of Deal Island Crab with Sour Cream		1.00
Backfire of Misdeal with Sour Alibi		.30
Deep Sea Scallops with Salty Accent		1.00
Back Bay Trollops with Harvard Accent		2.00 plus tip
English Sole Armenonville		.75
English Heel Newport		20.00

LANCASTER AND CHESTER
THE SPRINGMAID LINE

DI...

A La Cart...

E...

Steak Tartare with Raw Egg, Raw Onion, and Raw Gentian Violet	2.5
Cannibal Sandwich with real collar buttons	2.0
Bruised Brisket of Beef, from Salvage	2.0
hit by a Vice-President	3.0
Rump Steak with Sally Lund	1.
with Sally Rand	3.0
Top Round, Dagmar	3.5
Bottom Round, Gypsy Rose	4.0
Fricassee of Fabulous Fanny, Broad Gauge	6.0
Pork Chop stuffed with Apple	2.
Pork Barrel stuffed with Republican	3.
with Apple in Mouth	4.0
Mutton Chops stuffed with Union League	3.0
Cold Cuts, Junior League	2.0
Hot Dogs with Hush Puppies	
Hot Minks—Wild	200.0
Ranch	300.
White Mutation	400.
White House	.0
Grilled Railbirds with horseradish	5 to
Saddle of Mutton with Hot Popovers	2.0
with Hot Pushovers	20.0
Breast of Guinea Hen on Toast	2.5
Breast of Chicken on Television—each	3.5
Breast of Squab stuffed with Foam Rubber	
Breast of Peasant stuffed with Russian Propaganda	10 Rubl
Long Island Ugly Duckling stuffed with Turnip Greens and Pearl Onions	1.5
Lame Duck stuffed with Long Green and Perle Mesta	.5
Roast Spring Lamb with Garlic	1.2
Elliott Springs with Garlic and Chlorophyll	.1

YOU CAN'T GO WRO...

Menu printed as joke by a railroad, the Lancaster and Chester, which never had a passenger service.

NER
by Express

EES

THE HEART OF PEACHLAND

Drawn and Quartered Democrat Roasted in
   own Jacket 2.00

Sirloin of Beef with Marquis Potatoes
   New York 1.00
   Newport . . . . 15 shillings

Baron of Beef with Duchess Salad
   New York 1.00
   Palm Beach . . . . 1000 Lira

French Lamb Chops with Domestic Pants 1.50

Domestic Lamb Chops with Imported Pants . . . 1.50

Imported Mermaid without Pants 2.50

Leg of Lamb, Marilyn Monroe 2.50

Jerked Deer stewed in Chestnuts 1.50

Dear Jerk stewed in Chestnut Hill 20.00

Porterhouse Steak, Polonaise 3.00

Parkerhouse Rolls, Polly Adler 30

Imported Bustard stuffed with domestic snipe . . 3.00

Domestic Bastard stuffed with imported tripe . . .15

Young Whale stuffed with imported Jaguar . . 5000.00
        with Domestic Station Wagon   500.00

Left Wing of Young Turk stewed in own juice . . 50.00

Unicorn Steak with Lionnaise Potatoes . . . 2.00

Bear's Liver with Bacon 2.00

Bull's Liver with Halsey 2.00

Stewed Kidneys with Leeks, McKay 2.00

Chipped Beef 75

Chip Robert 30

Ham Hocks 75

Ham Fisher 30

Hollingshead, Salome 30

Philadelphia Scrapple with Blackeyed Peas . . .75

Washington Scramble with Pommes Cafritz . . .30

Boston Scrod 2.00

THE SPRINGMAID LINE

Vegetables

Alligator Pear 1.00
Pair of Alligators 2.00
Stewed Tomatoes, Dickens
        New York   20.00
        Palm Beach   40.00
Hopping John Reed King . . .30
Bell Peppers
   with Hothouse Stuffing . 1.00
   with Hotbox Stuffing . . .50
Apple Sauce to Lay
   The Golden Goose . . 1.00
Grady Cole Slaw 30
Candied Yams 80
Bandied Gams 1.80
Baked Potatoes in
   Sanforized Jackets . . .60

Desserts

Pie filled with Cheesecake
        Up to Here   .55
        Up to There   .65
Pie filled with Cup Custard
        Tete a Tete   .85
Pie filled with Fan Dancer
        New York   20.00
        Palm Beach   40.00
Biscuit Tortoni Hulman . . . 2.50
Hasty Pudding 15
Pot-de-Creme with French Rum 1.00
Rumpot with French Tarte . . 2.00
Peach, Melba 1.00
Cantaloupe, Lillian Russell . . 1.50
Watermelon, Jane Russell . . 2.00
Baked Sam Adams' Apple . . 1.00
Creole Paulines 20.00
Crepes Suzettes with
   Individual Pyrene . . . 2.00
Pitted Grapes 1.25
Potted Dates
        New York   20.00
        Palm Beach   40.00
New Orleans Coffee
   with U.all.no. Mints . . .80
Assorted Nuts 1.25
Nuts a Vous . . . . . Tax Free

7

Calendars, Posters, and
Advertising Memorabilia

T HE ART of chromolithography reached its zenith during the
last quarter of the nineteenth century, and railroad executives, long
experienced in the printing of millions of timetables, were quick to
see the advertising advantages of publishing colorful illustrated
calendars with pictures of their famous locomotives, scenery along
their routes, and babies and pretty girls. The collecting of railroad
calendars can be a never-ending hobby. There are thousands from
which to choose, and many represent the work of well-known
commercial artists of the late nineteenth and early twentieth
centuries.

Calendars as give-away promotional advertising of the railroads
seem to have lasted up to the present, and many collectors add new
ones to their collections each December, but the early color-litho-
graphed calendars are the prime collector's items. Time, of course,
was a subject that was uppermost in the minds of all railroad men,
and often a handsome calendar was the only Christmas present
given by the management to employees. Most desirable of all old
calendars are those that illustrate the famous steam locomotives of an

earlier day. While railroad calendars with illustrations other than trains are in some demand, those illustrated with train pictures are by far the most desirable.

Also of special interest are the novelty calendars devised to bring special attention to a certain railway's services. A perpetual calendar with a revolving disc was given away by the Cleveland Lorain and Wheeling Railway in 1896, and there is little doubt that this clever and complicated calendar was a strong departure in advertising giveaways in its time. Another novelty calendar in the shape of a mailbag was distributed in 1897 by the Lake Shore and Michigan Southern Railway. It is significant that these specially designed and printed calendars cost so little in their time that thousands could be printed in color and die-cut at little cost to the railroads.

Some railways offered a choice of calendar designs in the same year. Frequently these were made with designs that would have a regional appeal. Those who did not want to display the risqué calendar called "Summer Impressions," showing a couple attired in swimsuits, could choose a more demure illustration with fully clothed people.

The Great Rock Island Route gave away a "World's Fair Calendar" in 1892 to wish its passengers to Chicago Merry Christmas and Happy New Year, while reminding them "that quick time is made on the 'Great Rock Island' and the vestibuled reclining, dining, and sleeping cars are delightfully warm in the dead of winter." The same cars were just as warm in the dead of summer, too.

In 1899 the Sunset Limited between New Orleans and California ("The Land of Sunshine, Fruit and Flowers," according to the calendar) gave away an advertising calendar with an illustration of a cute nude baby reclining in comfort in a sleeping car. The message on the calendar urged the prospective passengers to get "away from this beastly weather to the MID-WINTER SUMMER-LAND, CALIFORNIA."

Closely associated with chromolithographed calendars are the railways' advertising posters of the period from around 1870 to 1920. There were thousands of these colorful posters printed, and while many were just general advertisements meant to entice passengers during a period of fierce competition between rival railroads, others advertised specific excursions or engineering developments of a railway system, such as the International Bridge

There is a footnote at the bottom of this 1899 calendar that reads "WABASH-Indian- a cloud blown forward by an equinoctial wind. Webster's Unabridged Dictionary."

Calendar for the year given to Norfolk and Western Railway employees as a Christmas gift. Message emphasizes company's interest in promoting safety.

Calendar for the year 1900, issued by the Nickel Plate Railroad, used patriotic theme in relating "a peerless trio of American admirals" (Farragut, Dewey, and Porter) to the line's "peerless trio of daily express trains" between Chicago and New York.

138

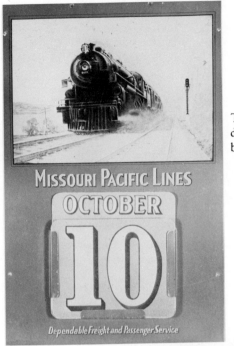

Tinplate calendar on which months and dates could be changed was given away by the Missouri Pacific Railroad.

Any material associated with railroading is collectible. This 1893 calendar for a western Pennsylvania resort is desirable because it shows a Pittsburgh, Fort Wayne and Chicago train at the depot next to the hotel.

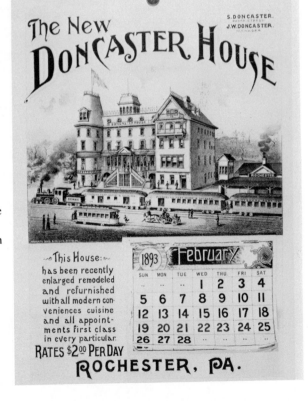

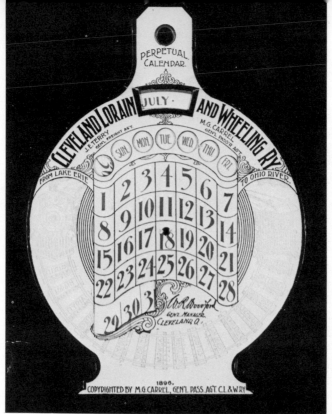

Perpetual calendar issued in 1896 by
the Cleveland Lorain and Wheeling
Railway.

The December 1892 leaf of the Rock
Island calendar reminds patrons that the
Chicago World's Fair starts the
following year and the Rock Island is
"the road to ride."

140

The Lake Shore and Michigan Southern Railway incorporated the fast mail theme in a great deal of its advertising. This pocket-sized 1897 calendar is cut and colored to simulate a U.S. mail pouch.

between Buffalo, New York, and Fort Erie, Canada. Engines, entire trains, and natural wonders were also used for poster illustration.

One of the most desirable calendar series is that which was given away by the New York Central Railroad. The calendars were illustrated with lithographs of paintings of trains and locomotives, and frequently the illustrations alone can be found today, attesting to the fact that the pictures were appreciated long after the calendar was out of date. Obviously many railroad men cut off the large train illustrations and saved them. Mint copies of these artistic calendar pictures are now expensive as collectors strive to put together the whole series with an example from each of the years in which they were printed.

From the number of railroad calendars that still survive, it is obvious that the railroads were more than willing to pay for calendars that would remind both their employees and customers that travel on advertised routes was comfortable, safe, and pleasant. A great variety of subject matter and designs was used on railroad calendars, and they represent an era when an excellent quality of color printing was available at low cost.

New York Central series of annual calendars used large colorful artwork of their crack passenger trains in action. In this one, the Empire State is traveling along the Hudson River across from West Point.

142

The association with Washington Irving's Rip Van Winkle was used to make traveling to the Catskill Mountains in New York attractive to patrons of the now long-defunct Ulster and Delaware Railroad.

Calendars were not, of course, the only advertising material used by the railroads to entice their customers. Small, colorfully printed trade cards were also a common giveaway, and unlike the calendars, most of which were thrown away at the end of the year, trade cards were often pasted into albums to be looked at on long winter nights. Sometimes these small cards were printed with an advertisement on one side and a calendar on the other, and were both artistic and practical.

Among the more permanent advertising items given by the railroads were glass paperweights and men's penknives. The insignia of the railroad was always clearly printed on them. All the older paperweights having photographic views of scenes along the route or a picture of a train belonging to the advertiser are in demand today.

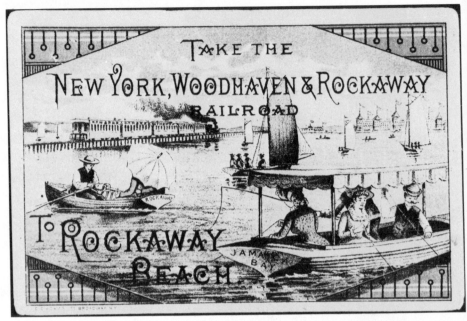

Turn-of-the-century trade card shows steam-powered train crossing Jamaica Bay, N. Y., on its way to Rockaway Beach resort. In the foreground is a fishing party, and beyond, a romantic couple under a parasol are being rowed around the bay.

Two prospectors look over the route of the Tonopah and Tidewater Railroad that ran from Los Angeles through Nevada mining territory.

144

Paperweight advertising Missouri Pacific Railway.

Rock Island paperweight.

Pocketknives issued as advertising items by railways.

There are literally hundreds of different glass and ceramic ashtrays bearing the insignia of America's railroads, and while these were not originally meant to be given away, it is probable that the railroad management assumed that the ashtrays would be stolen by passengers who wanted souvenirs of their trips and advertising on each of them would have some value.

Playing cards were also especially printed to advertise the railroads. The cards were usually sold to passengers who were looking for a way to pass the time on long trips. Railroad playing cards are considered collectible items by both card collectors and railroad buffs. Those cards most in demand are the decks on which are found photographic scenes of the more obscure routes or pictures of defunct lines or early trains.

Matchbook covers, colorfully printed with the logos of the trains of the past, are yet another category of advertising item that is collectible. Because these are relatively inexpensive, many collectors strive to find matchbook covers that represent as many rail lines and name trains as possible. Those that are illustrated with pictures of trains are particularly in demand.

Group of ashtrays used on trains. Management expected them to be stolen.

Ceramic ashtrays. Top photo is Illinois Central.

Card playing was a common pastime on long train trips, and the railroads sold decks in huge numbers. This is a selection of collectible playing cards, some with scenic views on their faces or backs, and a warning sign from the Pullman Company.

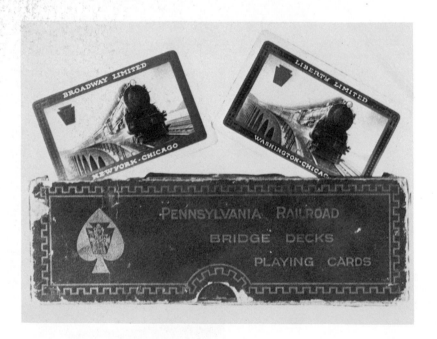

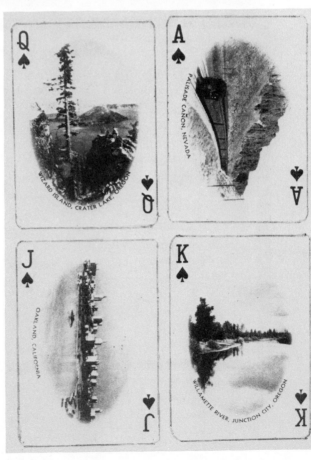

WARNING

The Pullman Company calls the attention of its patrons to the fact that "Card Sharks" and "Con Men" have started their winter campaign on railroad trains.

Passengers can protect themselves by refusing to play with strangers.

Railroad matchbook covers, while not very valuable, make a colorful and varied display when a large number of roads are represented.

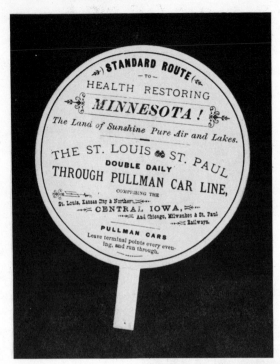

Without air conditioning, patrons of Pullman cars needed these free advertising fans.

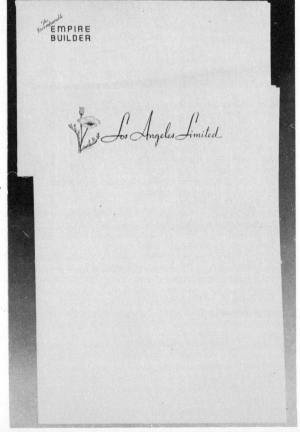

Specially designed and printed stationery was available to passengers on long trips. The railways understood the value of advertising.

152

Nineteenth-century sales folder for railroad hand car.

All advertising items issued by the railroads in the past are of some interest to railroad historians. Years ago railroads were willing to spend a lot of money to represent their lines as being safer, faster, and more enjoyable than any other mode of travel. Now that this is no longer true, collectors feel a special urge to preserve those items that represent a more leisurely method of travel.

153

Old advertising pieces showing trains or with railroading associations are part of railroadiana collecting.

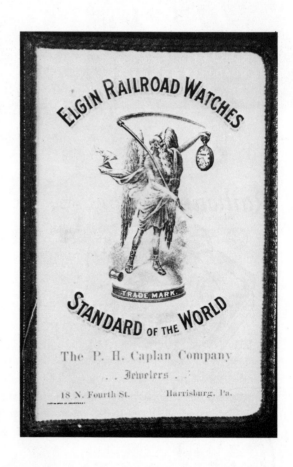

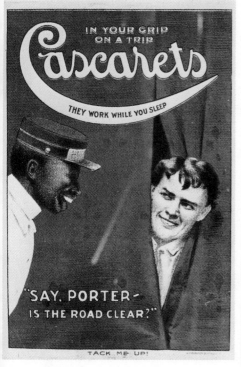

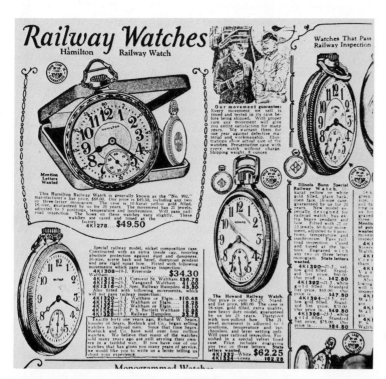

155

8

Books, Pulp Magazines, and Sheet Music

THE DEVELOPMENT of railroading in America opened up limitless possibilities for writers of fiction and nonfiction, and books and magazines that romanticized trains and the men who ran them appeared with increasing frequency. In October 1906, Volume I, Number 1 of the *Railroad Man's Magazine* appeared on the newsstand. Today it is a collector's item.

Many of the publications about railroaders and railroading were commissioned by railroad management and were straightforward histories of the lines with some propaganda included. Other railroad books were romanticized and fictionalized stories about the brave men who ran the trains and built the tracks. All these stories had one thing in common: they made heroes of the engineers, brakemen, switchmen, and conductors of the railroads, and they spurred young boys who read them with an ambition to work for the railroad. Railroad men became heroes of the late nineteenth century and the early part of this century. The romantic railroad books, both pulp and hardcover, appeared by the hundreds. Especially in the so-called dime novels (which sold for a nickel), the forerunner of American paperback books, could a young boy find escape in dreaming of the day when he, too, could become that most exciting of all heroes—the railway engineer. Stories of train robberies, mail robberies, train wrecks, fires, and other disasters always ended with the railroad employee triumphant. It's little wonder that the railroads seldom had any difficulty filling any jobs that were open.

The collector has a wide range of railroad literature from which to choose. Many of the pulp magazines were heavily illustrated with pictures of steam locomotives and a wide variety of railroad scenes. These illustrations, although far from technically accurate, are often vivid and help explain why working on the railroad was the perfect fantasy occupation for any all-American boy. When the young reader dreamed of running away, it was usually either to join the circus or to work on a train.

For the railroading bibliophile there are many hardcover books from which to choose. Illustrations for some of these books were done by the leading artists of the late-nineteenth and early-twentieth centuries. Again, although the illustrations are often far from technically accurate, they are impressions worth keeping. Old books about railroads can generally be divided into two categories: those written for children and those for adults. Many of them have handsome turn-of-the-century covers, and while some were published by the country's leading publishers and were meant for public distribution, others that have a close connection with a particular early railroad line were commissioned. A few of the old books are autobiographical stories of railroad men's experiences.

If one were to believe the stories in the early pulps, there was never a dull moment on the early trains, and opportunities for heroism arose at least every five miles. A wonderful series of dime novels, published between 1898 and 1906 and called Pluck and Luck, Complete Stories of Adventure, had titles such as *Rob Ralston's Run or The Perilous Career of a Boy Engineer*; *Sixty Mile Sam or Bound to be on Time*; *Engineer Steve, The Prince of the Rail*. The covers of these books illustrated the high point of each tale, the details of which could be found within the fragile covers. Excitement was always at a peak in these stories, which had such sentences as, "The express was in sight when young Rob sprang forward, leaped up into the cart, seized the girl in his arms and jumped. Almost as soon as his feet touched the ground the cart was splintered

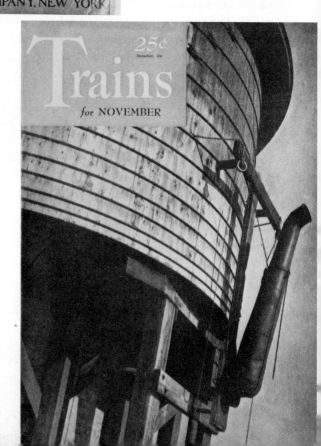

Covers of the first issue of the
Railroad Man's Magazine, issued
in October 1906, and of *Trains*,
November 1940.

ST NICHOLAS

THE·CENTURY·CO·353·FOURTH·AVE·NEW·YORK

Any magazine cover with a good train illustration is collectible.

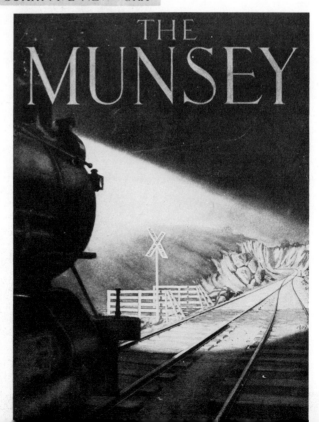

THE MUNSEY

Around the turn of the century so-called dime novels sold for a nickel. Collectors seek those with colorful covers illustrating railroad stories.

160

COMRADES

Tales of Adventure for Young Folks

No. 23. Price, Five Cents.

TOM WRIGHT'S COMRADES
OR THE GIRL FIREMAN OF ENGINE 66

BY ROBERT STEEL

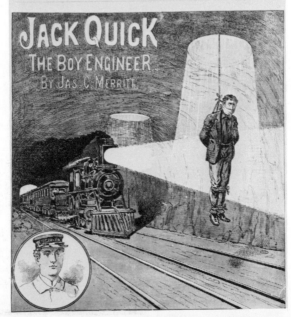

PLUCK AND LUCK

COMPLETE STORIES OF ADVENTURE.

No. 20. NEW YORK, OCTOBER 5, 1898. Price 5 Cents.

JACK QUICK
THE BOY ENGINEER.
BY JAS. C. MERRITT.

CONFESSIONS
OF A RAILROAD
SIGNALMAN

JAMES O. FAGAN

All books with railroading
subjects are sought by collectors.
This group published between
1884 and 1925 is especially
desirable.

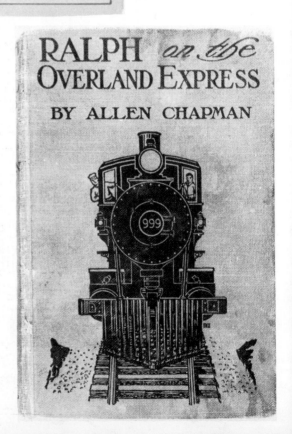

RALPH *on the*
OVERLAND EXPRESS
BY ALLEN CHAPMAN

999

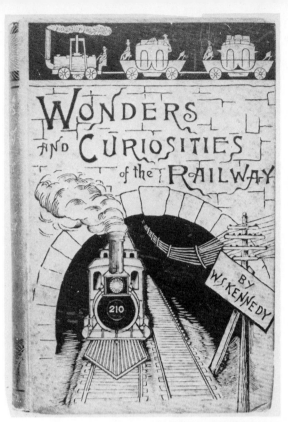

WONDERS AND CURIOSITIES of the RAILWAY
BY W.S.KENNEDY

The GREAT K&A TRAIN ROBBERY

by
PAUL LEICESTER FORD
Author of JANICE MEREDITH

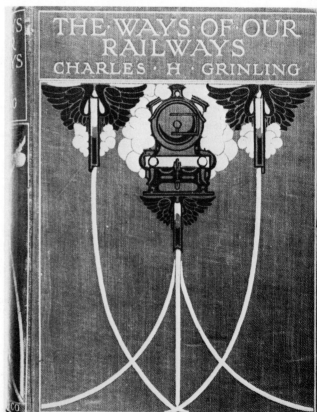

164

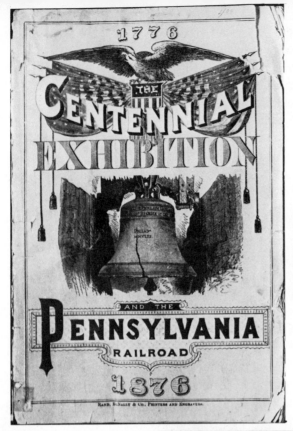

Booklet published by the Pennsylvania Railroad in 1876; it includes a description of the Centennial Exhibition in Philadelphia and the routes and services of the railroad.

The July 1868 issue of the *Pinkerton Detective Series*, a monthly magazine that was an early forerunner of the Nick Carter, Pluck and Luck, and Brave and Bold series.

and the horse instantly slain." Certainly, this type of adventure tale was enough to encourage any boy to want to work for the railroad.

Perhaps one of the most desirable books on railroading for today's enthusiasts is *The American Railway* published by Charles Scribner's Sons in 1888. The book is a collection of essays written by men who were in railroad management or edited railway journals. Taken together the essays form a fairly complete picture of railroading history up to the time that the book was published. The state of railroad technology is rather well covered, and in addition, and perhaps just as important for railroadiana fans, the book is illustrated with over two hundred engravings of various railway scenes, equipment, and personnel. The text offers a rather prejudiced view of railroad labor during the late nineteenth century, and there are many less than flattering references to the men who worked for the railroad companies. For instance, one writer writes, "Brakemen have the reputation of doing a good deal of flirting" and "The switch-tender, whose momentary carelessness has many times caused terrible disaster. . . ." The writer does conclude, however, that "railroad men as a body are industrious, sober when at work,

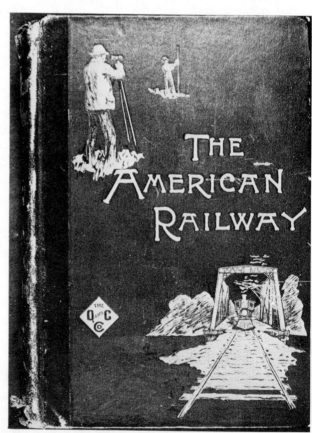

The American Railway, published by Scribner's in 1893, was a collection of essays on railroad operations by various railroad company executives. It is a very thorough discussion of railroading problems and operating techniques from management's point of view.

166

and lively when at play, using well-trained minds, in their sphere, and possessing capacity for a high degree of further training."

All early books on railroading, whether fiction or fact, are of interest to specialist-collectors. Many search for complete runs of the *Railroad Man's Magazine* or copies of *Work and Win* and *Pluck and Luck* that featured adventure stories of railroad men.

Other collectible literature are the manuals dealing with the operation and maintenance of all railroading equipment from locomotives to signals. These help the rail buff to understand how the equipment was made and how it operated. Also of interest are the nineteenth-century compilations of detailed railroad information contained in the *Manual of the Railroads of the United States*, which was an annual publication.

Locomotives and trains have inspired the writing of many popular songs and much dance and country music since well before the Civil War. Many of the covers on published sheet music have contemporary illustrations of artistic as well as historical importance, and all sheet-music covers with illustrations of railroad trains, elevated trains, or trolleys are collected along with other examples of railroadiana. Collectors look, in particular, for any piece of sheet music with the picture of a train on the cover.

Pre-Civil War sheet-music covers are superb examples of the lithographer's art, and these earliest items are rare and somewhat expensive. Railroad music dates from around 1828 in America, and it was published in Baltimore, Philadelphia, Boston, and New York. A few of the pieces of sheet music that can be found from the early period were hand colored over the lithographed pictures, and these are considered to be the gems of early sheet-music illustration.

Probably the most valuable of all early railroad music is "The Rail Road," composed by C. Meineke and published by John Cole of Baltimore in 1828. It is the first sheet-music cover to have railway mail as a subject, and the engraving was done by J. Sands. The illustration is a comical engraving showing a vehicle called the "Ohio Velocipede"; there are several passengers about to embark and a group of friends seeing them off. Within balloons, which predate the comic-strip form of printing dialogue today, are these speeches: "Give my love to all my nine Cousins and tell Aunt Polly that I'll drink tea with her in Cincinnati tomorrow evening and bring the new bonnet and the gigot pattern and the Flounces and

BOSTON AND MAINE RAILROAD

Rules Applicable to Employes in Station, Telegraph and Signal Tower Service

and

Wage Table

EFFECTIVE MARCH 18, 1927

Railroad company rule books, equipment operating instruction manuals, rate guides, and official reports contain a great deal of information for serious collectors.

NEW YORK ONTARIO & WESTERN RAILWAY COMPANY

RULES OF THE OPERATING DEPARTMENT

MAY 15, 1913

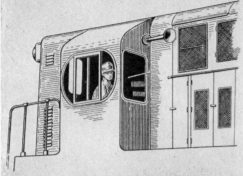

FAIRBANKS-MORSE

ALL PURPOSE AND
HEAVY DUTY
LOCOMOTIVES

OPERATOR'S
TROUBLE SHOOTING
MANUAL

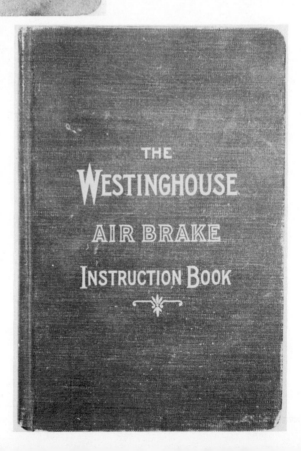

THE
WESTINGHOUSE
AIR BRAKE
INSTRUCTION BOOK

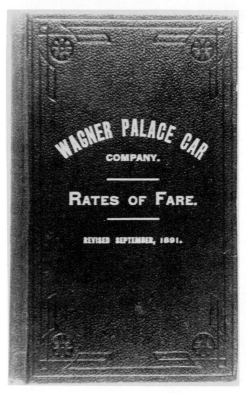

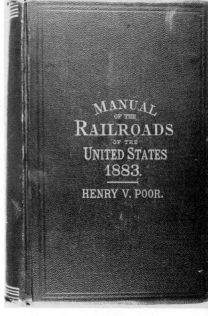

Pre-Civil War sheet-music cover has both a railroading and abolitionist theme.

All"; "Don't forget to drop my letter in the Post Office at Wheeling so it may get to N. Orleans the next day." This particular piece of illustrated railway music has always been a desirable item for all sheet-music collectors and is not easily found today.

George Willig of Baltimore published the "Rail Road March" in 1828. The cover tells us that the piece was written "For the Fourth of July," and was dedicated "to the Directors of the Baltimore and Ohio Rail Road." C. Meineke also wrote this music and the lithographed cover has an illustration of a flying eagle holding two shields in his beak. Underneath is an early engine, a tender, and three cars. An engineer stands on one side of the engine, and a fireman sits on the front of the tender.

"Ranger's Trip to Westborough" was published in 1834 in Boston by S. Bradlee. The music was composed by James Hooton. It commemorates the opening of the railroad to Westborough, Massachusetts, on November 15, 1834, and the cover illustration shows troops in front of a small building marked "hotel." The troops are waiting to embark on railway coaches, and there is a large figure of a lion facing the hotel.

In 1845 A. Fiot of Philadelphia published "The Alsacian Rail Road Gallops," which were written by J. Guignard. The lithographed cover by Duval from a drawing by S. Schmitz shows a view of Philadelphia with a building marked "Piano Forte Warehouse," which was probably the establishment of the publisher. Below are twelve railroad coaches coupled to an engine, tender, and one baggage car. The tops of the notes in the left hand of the piano part serve as tracks in the picture.

Another early example of sheet music with railroad illustrations on the cover is "Fast Line Gallop" composed by Jas. N. Back and published by Lee and Walker of Philadelphia in 1853. At the head of the title is printed, "To the President and Directors of the Great Pennsylvania Central R.R." The lithography was done by Fritz and Derleth of St. Louis, and the illustration has in the center a railroad map covering the area from the Atlantic seacoast to the western edge of Illinois, Kentucky, and Virginia and North to Canada. At the bottom is a view of the Susquehanna viaduct, showing a railroad bridge with two trains. At the left, right, and bottom of the view are tables of "Distances from Cleveland-Cincinnati-Ohio River" with mileage.

A march for the pianoforte, "Northern Route," written by C. C. Smith, was published by William A. Pond in New York in 1876. The cover illustration has a small bridge tender, one freight car, and three coaches passing through a stone arch. The cover was engraved by Stackpole, and the music is dedicated to Mr. Fred Taylor, President, Burlington & Northern Railway.

"The Iron Horse" is a song that was published by Lee & Walker of Philadelphia in 1870, with music by Alfred von Rochow and words by Harry Frances. It was dedicated to the Brotherhood of Locomotive Engineers, and the cover engraving by G. F. Swain shows an engine and tender marked "Moses Taylor."

A later item that illustrates an early nostalgia for the old trains is "The Limited Express Train March," which, although published in 1894, has an engraving of the first railroad train in America in 1827. "The Grand Trunk Waltzes" has a cover illustration of a train crossing the Grand Trunk Railroad Bridge over the St. Lawrence River, and this piece was published in New York by William Hall and Son in 1854. An 1867 item, "Blue Line Gallop," has an illustration of a freight car of the Michigan Central Railroad and music titled "Harnden's Express Line Gallopade & Trio" has a Firth and Hall lithograph of the pioneer express line between New York and Boston in 1841. An illustration of the "Cape Horn Placer Company, California, and the Sierra Nevada of the line of the Pacific Railroad" can be found on the cover of "New Express Galop," published in 1869.

Another song dedicated to the Brotherhood of Locomotive Engineers in 1895 was "My Dad's the Engineer," published by Henry J. Wehman. The cover illustration shows a steam engine with an inset of passengers in a coach car. "A Message on the Train," published in 1897, has an illustration of a scene in a club car on the North West Limited.

"The Great Rock Island Route" is a musical piece published in 1880, and the cover illustration shows a passenger depot in Chicago and a small picture of the approach to the Sierras. "The Q Galop," published by John Church and Company in 1884, shows on its cover a Chicago, Burlington and Quincy railroad train crossing a bridge.

Even more scarce than early railroad sheet music is music written for elevated trains or trolleys, but some examples do exist. "Rapid

The skating scene in Pittsburgh, Pa., on the 1865 sheet-music cover shows both a steam-powered passenger train and a horse-drawn trolley.

"Bicycle Glide" cover, published in 1880, shows a steam locomotive on a bridge crossing the Schuylkill River in Philadelphia.

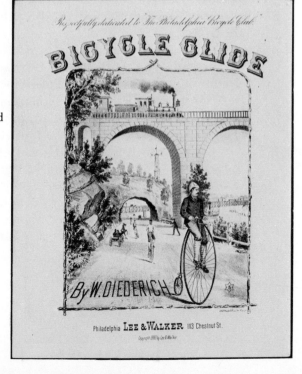

Transit Galop," published in Philadelphia by F. A. North in 1875, has a cover illustration of a Philadelphia street scene with an elevated train in transit. An important trolley item is "Highland Grand March." It was "dedicated to the Officers of the Highland Street Railway Company" and was written in 1877. The cover shows two horse-drawn trolleys—one a double-decker—with passengers on the Highland Street Railway in Boston.

"Seeing Denver" has a cover with a photographic illustration of passengers in an observation car of the Denver Trolley Line in 1906, and "Take a Car," published in 1905, has an illustrated cover of a couple boarding a street car. Another song, written the same year, is "Upon the Trolley Line," and the cover has an illustration of an electric trolley.

The earliest publication of the best-known of all railroad songs, "I've Been Working on the Railroad," will probably surprise all railroad buffs. The song was first printed under the title "Levee Song" in the eighth edition of *Carmina Princetonia* on page 24. However, later editions of the music with the more familiar title can be found with railroad illustrations on the cover. The same music is now used for the song "The Eyes of Texas."

While the above are all early and rather scarce examples of railroad songs and musical pieces, there are many later railroad songs that can still be found in some quantity, although due to the popularity of collecting any "transportation music" these also are becoming scarce. One of the best-known pieces of railroad sheet music is "Casey Jones." This piece was first published in 1909, and the comic ballad made a hero out of a rather foolhardy employee of the railroad.

"All Aboard for Blanket Bay" is a 1910 railroad hit, and in 1921 "De Gospel Train" was published. An interesting popular song that is relatively unknown today is "Pullman Porters on Parade" written in 1913 by Irving Berlin but published under the name of "Ren. G. May" which is an anagram for Germany.

All train buffs are aware of the 1896 ballad by Gussie L. Davis, "In the Baggage Coach Ahead," and certainly the 1912 hit by Irving Berlin, "When the Midnight Choo-Choo Leaves for Alabam" is a collectible item. Those who grew up in the 1940's will surely remember Johnny Mercer's "On the Atchison, Topeka and the Santa Fe," Sunny Skylar's and Martin Block's "Waiting For the Train to Come In," and, of course, "Chattanooga Choo-Choo."

All railroading songs are collectible, especially when a train is illustrated on the sheet-music cover. The "Give Me the Moon Over Brooklyn" cover, on page 178, is of interest because of its night view of New York City's elevated railway and trolley cars.

Obviously the above are only a few of the more desirable collectible railroad songs and music. Throughout their history, the railroads inspired a large group of musical pieces and songs, and these, in turn, inspired engravers, artists, lithographers, and photographers to record on the covers of the sheet music the way the railroads looked at the time the music was written. Thus the music becomes a pictorial history of the development of American railroading. In addition to the published music, there are many railroad buffs who realize that there are numerous folk songs that were never published, and some effort has been made in the past few years to record this country music before it is forgotten.

9

Picture Postcards

SOME OF the most valuable documentation of early railroad history can be found on the hundreds of thousands of picture postcards made before and after the turn of the century. The postcards were sold in train depots or peddled on trains by candy butchers. On many trains they were given away free as advertisements by the railroads. One very collectible category, which was never given away by the railroads and was not apt to be found in depot racks, is the disaster card that illustrates a train accident or wreck.

Railroad postcards can generally be divided into the following categories: pictures of trains; pictures of depots; pictures of railroad-car interiors, illustrating the comfort and luxury to be found on particular trains; pictures of the scenery to be enjoyed along a particular route; and pictures of railroad disasters. Many collectors search for cards that depict all the depots that once stood in a particular geographical area. Others search for pictures of steam locomotives or the later name trains and streamliners. Still other collectors try to assemble all the picture postcards representing trains and depots of just one rail line, preferably one that is no longer functioning. Trolley cars are another category of postcards that has great appeal for railroad buffs.

Most railroad postcards are photographic and are fascinating examples of the photographer's art at a time when cameras and equipment were primitive and heavy. Many were made before color photography was possible, and these are hand-colored over black and white pictures.

Few train disasters seem to have taken place that went unrecorded by local photographers, who managed to set up their tripods almost

Oncoming trains make spectacular views for picture postcards. Upper photo is of B & O Royal Blue Limited, Baltimore, Md.; lower photo is of New York-St. Louis Express No. 65 leaving Cumberland, Md.

Postcard showing opera star Fritzi Scheff leaving train of
the Atlanta and West Point Railroad named in her honor.

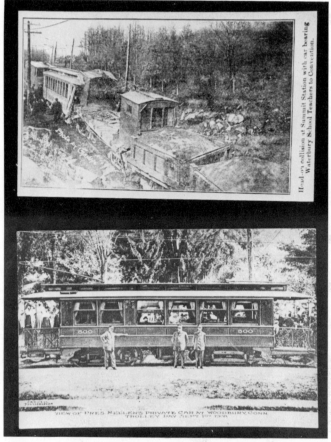

All train and trolley disasters were recorded on postcards. Upper
photo shows "Head-on collision at Summit Station with car
bearing Waterbury [Conn.] School Teachers to Convention."
Lower photo shows "View of Pres. Mellen's Private Car at
Woodbury, Conn. Trolley Day, Sept. 1st, 1908."

124-. Trolley Accident, Nov. 29, 1907. Trolley containing 29 passengers, struck by a pair of Locomotives on West Main Street Crossing, Waterbury, Conn.

Picture postcards showing two trolley accidents in Connecticut in early 1900's.

TROLLEY CAR wrecked at Seymour, Conn., Dec. 26, 1909, down 50 ft. bank into Rimmon Pond. Photo taken directly after accident, while crew were still in the car. Photo by Geo. Ford, Seymour, Conn. (Copyrighted 1910 by Geo. Ford.)

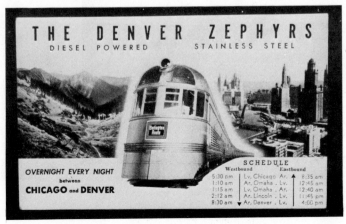

Picture postcard giving schedule of streamliners on the Burlington Route's Chicago and Denver line.

183

before rescue teams went to work to extricate the passengers and crew. The reason for this is that the photographer who was fortunate enough to get to the scene early was able to sell his picture to a postcard company and to newspapers. Disaster postcards sold rapidly and in quantity, and many photographers earned their living photographing local scenes and especially fires and accidents for postcard reproduction. The postcards were then pasted carefully in albums, so that the train or trolley wreck could be remembered and discussed at length in later years.

Picture postcards are the best record we have today of depot architecture. During the height of train travel in the United States, depots were built at a rapid rate and became more and more elaborate. Many old depots have now been torn down, and only the

Depot and Harvey House in Sapulpa, Okla.

Postcard showing Osipee, N.H., depot with gingerbread architecture.

picture postcards remain to show us the wide range in architectural styles that prevailed in depot design. The depots represented the great variety of national and regional styles of architecture prevalent in the last half of the nineteenth century. The depot in Bemis, Maine, was styled like a log cabin; mission architecture was used in the West; and it was not unusual to find useless turrets, crenelated roofs, and fortlike buildings. Later depots, such as the Santa Fe in Oklahoma City, represent the Art Deco style of the 1920's and 1930's.

The railroads were somewhat daring in choosing architectural styles for depots and stations and seemed to spare little expense in building monuments that were more showy than functional. As the stations became obsolete and too expensive to keep up, they were torn down with little sentiment or regard for their value as architectural monuments to the great days of railroading. Most notable of the buildings that were lost in this way was the old Pennsylvania Station in New York City. Conservationists now realize the value in preserving what is left, and railroad stations and depots that seemed doomed to face the wrecker's ball are being saved and uses are being found for depots that might otherwise have been left to rot.

Collectors of railroadiana, meanwhile, have been preserving picture files of all depots, most of which were recorded on picture postcards. These cards give us a rather complete record of all the railroad buildings that connected the rail lines across the continent. In addition, the postcards also are a record of the great variety in rolling stock owned by the railways.

S. P. DEPOT, SAN ANTONIO, TEXAS.

Mission architecture of San Antonio depot in Texas.

185

Depot postcard of Bemis, Maine, illustrates unusual log
cabin architecture.

Art Deco architecture of the 1930's used for depot of Santa
Fe at Oklahoma City.

Postcard showing views of Pennsylvania Railroad tunnels
under the Hudson River.

Postcards showing exterior and interior views of Pennsylvania Station in New York that has been torn down.

Postcard showing Chicago railroad station with newer station in foreground and old exterior in back.

Postcard shows view of Union Station in San Bernardino, Calif.

Postcard showing first trolley car in Thomaston, Conn., in 1908.

7 A.M. to 6 P.M. Will write when I get located. Kindest regards to your wife + Lois

Ted —

ILLINOIS TRACTION

These are great cars + put the Pullman Co. in the shade

PEORIA—ST. LOUIS SLEEPING CAR ON THE "ROAD OF GOOD SERVICE"

Illinois Traction Company issued this postcard to advertise its sleeping-car trolley.

Trolley on postcard is overloaded with students headed for football game in Yale Bowl in New Haven, Conn.

10

Immigrant Material

IN ORDER TO ENCOURAGE the building and financing of railroads west of the Mississippi River to the Pacific Ocean, the United States Congress was badgered, bribed, and blackmailed into granting vast tracts of government-owned land to the railroads. The railroad lobbyists were able to convince the legislators that without this subsidy they would be unable to afford to purchase the required rights-of-way and to attract investment capital.

The amount of land given to the railroads in this manner totaled more than 242,000 square miles, larger than the entire country of France. Owning the land was important to the railroads, but more crucial was the need to develop and populate it and to sell some of it to pay for the costly building programs.

To accomplish this, the railroads sent agents to foreign ports of embarkation in Germany, Sweden, England, and elsewhere to induce new immigrants to buy land and settle in the Western states. Railroad representatives were also active in the larger American ports luring the fresh arrivals westward with promises of fertile farmland that could be bought for a few dollars an acre on easy credit terms.

Small promotional leaflet, printed by Wisconsin Central Railroad in late nineteenth century, simulating a piece of cut timber. View of homesteader's log cabin and message on back was employed to promote immigration to lands owned or served by the railroad.

Guide to land in Minnesota owned by the Northern Pacific Railroad. This pamphlet was distributed at an exposition in Vienna, Austria, in 1873 to encourage European emigration.

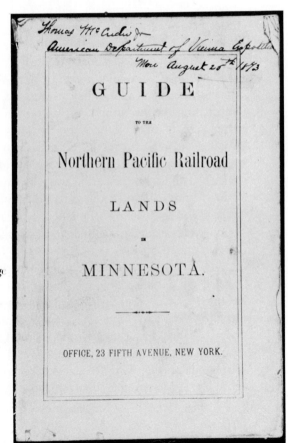

191

All of this salesmanship and proselytizing by the railroads is documented in the railroad collectibles relating to immigration to the West and the railroads' part in its promotion. We find among these relics such items as an 1885 timetable issued by the St. Paul, Minneapolis and Manitoba Railway which referred to itself as the Red River Valley Line. The striking outer cover of this timetable illustrates two steam-powered passenger trains traveling in opposite directions over what the caption describes as the "St.P.M.&M.Ry Double Track Stone Arch Bridge Minneapolis, Minn." In the background is seen the bustling, built-up commercial districts of the Twin Cities with tall chimneys spewing smoke to indicate a high level of industrial activity. At the bottom of the front cover James J. Hill, who went on later to put together the system that eventually became The Great Northern, heads the list of officers as President.

The back cover devotes two full pages to extolling the value to farmers of the government and railroad lands along its routes that were being "offered to citizens and intended citizens at a nominal cost that renders them practically FREE are reached only by the St. Paul, Minneapolis & Manitoba Railway." The copy goes on to point out that "the land-grant roads in the West and Southwest have, during the past years, by a most extravagant distribution of advertising matter, attracted a large immigration from Europe and elsewhere to their sections of the country, but now the Union Pacific and other roads have withdrawn all outside agencies and given public notice that they have 'no more agriculture land for sale.'" The folder then points out that the lands for sale by the St. Paul, Minneapolis and Manitoba Railway and the government land adjacent to its lines in Minnesota and northeastern Dakota are the only good, vacant agricultural lands of considerable size still available in the United States.

An interesting booklet concerned with selling land either controlled by a railroad or near to its right-of-way is a publication entitled *The Emigrant Guide or Hand-Book of the Wabash, St. Louis & Pacific Railway Company.* Printed on the cover is the following copy, "Great Inducements offered in Thrifty Towns to Homeseekers, and Choice Lands at Low Prices to the Farmer and Emigrant on this New Road." At the bottom of the cover page is this line, "Homes for the Homeless and Superior Locations for Capitalists and other Business Men."

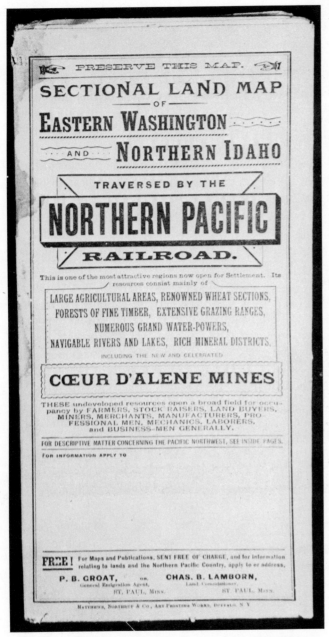

Land map of the area of eastern Washington and northern Idaho
served by the Northern Pacific Railroad. Like most literature
directed to immigrants cover copy extolls virtues of the land
available for settlement.

Front and back cover of St. Paul, Minneapolis and Manitoba Railway timetable.
Hard-sell message on back cover is directed to prospective land buyers.

THE immense emigration to the "Red River Valley" in Minnesota, and to Northeastern Dakota, and the absorption of government land by actual settlers during the past four years, has been noted as something unprecedented in the history of the settlement of any of the States or Territories of the West. The rapid development of this section of the country in so short a time, from that of an almost unoccupied waste to one of population and wealth, is attributed to the richness of its soil, its adaptability for profitable culture, its healthful climate, and other recognized advantages for settlement. The immigration still continues, and there is now every reason for the assurance that it will increase very largely the coming year.

The land-grant roads in the West and Southwest have, during the past years, by a most extravagant distribution of advertising matter, attracted a large immigration from Europe and elsewhere to their sections of the country, but now the Union Pacific and other roads have withdrawn all outside agencies, and given public notice that they have "no more agricultural lands for sale."

The land-grant roads of Iowa, and in Southern Minnesota have long since disposed of their lands, and the government lands tributary to those roads are all taken. The Northern Pacific road has disposed of nearly all of its agricultural lands in Minnesota, and the greater part of its lands in Eastern Dakota, and most of the government land near the road has also been disposed of.

The railroad lands now for sale by the St. Paul, Minneapolis & Manitoba Railway Company in Minnesota, the government lands still open for occupancy along and near its lines in the State, and the vast territory of vacant government land in Northeastern Dakota, made accessible by the late extension of the lines of this road, are to-day the only vacant good agricultural lands, in any considerable bodies, that can be found in the United States.

This important fact should be borne in mind by all who are seeking new lands, and all such will save time and money by writing direct to the offices of this Company for information.

FARMERS

WHO have to force from the exhausted or ungenerous soil of older settled States a scanty and precarious living, will do well to remember that as the result of the extent to which the public lands of the United States have been disposed of during the last few years — nearly

100,000,000 ACRES,

exclusive of railroad lands, HAVING PASSED FROM THE PUBLIC DOMAIN SINCE 1878 — the time is rapidly approaching when land, suitable for general farming and stock raising purposes, will no longer be obtainable, except by direct purchase from its fortunate possessor.

It is by no means unlikely that that unfortunate state of things — unfortunate at least for those who have not availed themselves of the opportunity to "catch on" before it was too late — may be hastened by the repeal of the U. S. Land Laws, which various circumstances are combining to bring about.

In the meantime there are

6,000,000 ACRES

of Government Land, positively the choicest in the entire Territory of Dakota, in the Devils Lake Land District, which includes the Turtle Mountain and Mouse River, with the intervening country.

Every day the amount is growing less, and under no circumstances will such valuable public lands long remain open to settlement.

These lands, offered to citizens and intended citizens at a nominal cost that renders them practically

FREE,

are reached only by the St. Paul, Minneapolis & Manitoba Railway.

Information regarding Rates and Routes to the Red River Valley, and all points in Northern Dakota, will be cheerfully furnished by any one of the following Agents of the Company:

H. F. McNALLY, General Traveling Agent, 28 East Front Street, TORONTO, CANADA.
J. M. HUCKINS, Traveling Agent, 28 East Front Street, TORONTO, CANADA.
E. C. LAWRENCE, Passenger Agent, 54 Clark Street, CHICAGO.
S. L. WARREN, New-York and New England Pass'r Ag't, 495 Broadway, ALBANY, N. Y.
E. P. ALLEN, Traveling Agent, 495 Broadway, ALBANY, N. Y.
RAY ALLEN, Traveling Agent, 412 Market Street, HARRISBURGH, PA.
D. W. H. MORELAND, Traveling Agent, 153 Jefferson Avenue, DETROIT, MICH.
ED. FISHBACK, Traveling Agent, INDIANAPOLIS, IND.
A. W. BROWNING, Traveling Agent, 54 Clark Street, CHICAGO, ILL.
WM. ABEL, Traveling Agent, Post-office Box 325, MILWAUKEE, WIS.
E. G. JAFFRAY, Traveling Agent, DES MOINES, IOWA.

— OR —

C. H. WARREN,   -   Gen'l Pass'r Ag't, St. P., M. & M. R'y, ST. PAUL, MINN.

195

Inside the brochure the text is devoted to describing the advantages and ambience of the various counties along the route. The numerous advertisements are taken by grain and feed dealers, hotels, clothiers, and undertakers. The largest ads were placed by land sales companies, such as the one by the Western Improvement Company of Iowa which offered "Town Lots and Valuable Real Estate" for "ONE-HALF CASH, Balance in Twelve Months." This company was apparently owned by the Wabash, St. Louis and Pacific Railway as all inquiries and payments could be addressed to any station agent of the line.

Other interesting relics of this period of western expansion are the guides to railroad lands published by the various rail lines and the maps which were as much promotional as geographic in their appeal. One such is the sectional land map of "Eastern Washington and Northern Idaho traversed by the Northern Pacific Railroad." On the front cover is printed:

This is one of the most attractive regions now open for settlement. Its resources consist mainly of

LARGE AGRICULTURAL AREAS, RENOWNED WHEAT SECTIONS,
FORESTS OF FINE TIMBER, EXTENSIVE GRAZING RANGES,
NUMEROUS GRAND WATER-POWERS, NAVIGABLE RIVERS AND LAKES,
RICH MINERAL DISTRICTS, including the new and celebrated COEUR D'ALENE MINES.

The railroads also offered special low-cost fares and excursion plans to prospective land buyers. This is evidenced by an 1890 brochure put out by the Iron Mountain Route advertising "½ Rate Home-Seekers' Excursions to Arkansas." The notice reads further: "Tickets good for thirty days. Stop-over privileges for the inspection of land allowed within the State." We also find a Missouri Pacific Railway Company ticket issued in 1906 as a "Special Homeseekers' Excursion Ticket, Good for ONE FIRST CLASS Passage to Pocatello, Idaho, And Return." Stop-overs up to fifteen days were permitted on this reduced-rate ticket.

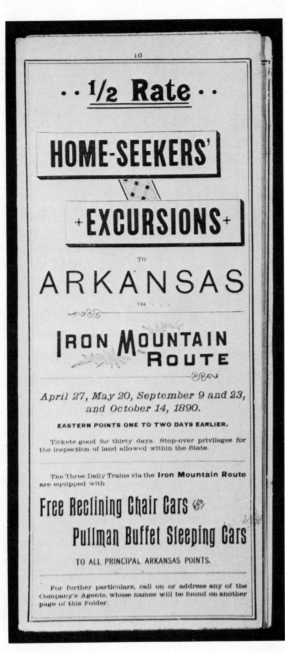

Folder of 1890 advertising cut-rate fares to Arkansas to promote land sales.

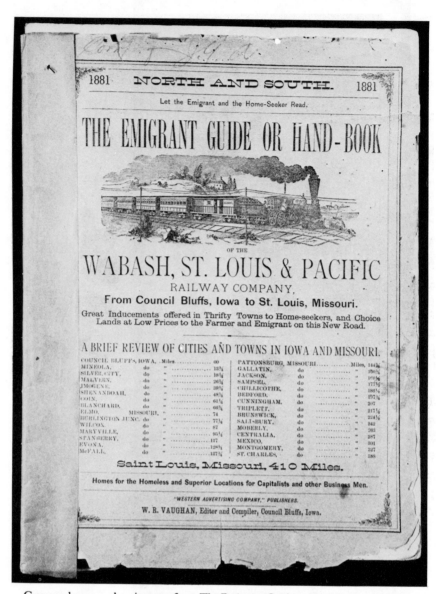

Cover and page 3 advertisement from *The Emigrant Guide or Hand-Book* published by Wabash, St. Louis and Pacific Railway in 1881 to induce settlement on railroad land.

the investment of capital in manufacturing and other enterprises.

There are two express, mail and freight trains passing Blanchard daily, making connections with trains going to Chicago, New York city, San Francisco, or any point to which you may wish to go. A branch road west is a sure thing and will open into the fertile fields of that productive country so that farmers, merchants grain and stock dealers may have free access to their shipping over the Main line of the Wabash, which makes through connections from the Atlantic to the Pacific.

As a general thing, the farms in this county are not extraordinarily large, a large share of our land being under cultivation, and nearly all of it under fence. One other item in favor of this county is that there are no large bodies of land held by speculators. Our farmers are generally supplied with abundance of stock water and where streams do not afford sufficient, it is easily obtained by digging wells, from twelve to twenty-five feet deep. Our farms vary in value from ten to forty dollars per acre, the amount of improvement and buildings thereon, location and other considerations, rather than character of the soil, which is universally good, controlling the price.

As a dairying and stock county, it will soon occupy a leading one. The fine pasturage on the uplands during summer and in the valleys earlier and later in the season, the ease with which the prairie sod can be converted into blue-grass pasture without cultivation, the adaptability of the soil to successfully produce the tame grasses, such as timothy, hungarian and millet, also corn, small grains and vegetables essential to increase milk production, the abundance of running streams, the numerous locations for dairy farms which nature has beautifully supplied, the small cost and easy terms on which they can be secured; these combined with the fine climate make this an unexcelled dairy region, commanding, as it does, a home market for dairy produce, for many years, and an unlimited one in the west.

We invite the attention of cheese makers to the many advantages offered by this county, near Blanchard, for successful dairy farming—especially those who own or hare to buy land worth over $100 per acre, where they have to feed several months longer each season, combine lower advantages and have no better if as good markets.

All the advantages of eastern civilization and society can be obtained in Blanchard. The orders of Masonry, Odd Fellows, Good Templars and Farms of Husbandry, have members located here who are every ready to extend the hand of welcome to the wandering brother. New dwelling houses and store buildings are springing up almost weekly, and carpenters command the best of wages. Nearly or quite one hundred thousand dollars worth of taxable property, in new buildings and houses have been added to the city during the past six months. From two to three hundred children attend school regularly, preparing themselves for the active future which awaits them, and one or two fine school buildings must and will soon be erected for their comfort.

The great want of Blanchard is manufactories. Paper mill, flax mill, oil mill, foundry, machine shops, etc., would all pay well. Situated in one of the best agricultural districts in the West, which now depends almost entirely upon eastern manufactories for its implements and farm machinery at a large cost with its railroad

3

Poster from 1858 of the Toledo Wabash and Great Western Railroad advertises only one change of cars between Toledo and St. Louis. Poster has note directed to Kansas emigrants

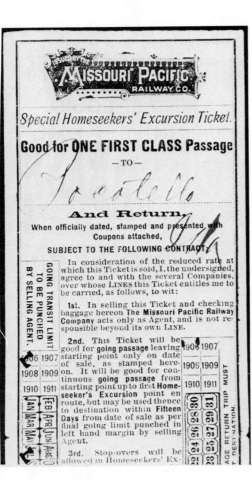

Portion of 1906 Missouri Pacific Railway reduced-fare ticket to Pocatello, Idaho, sold to persons seeking homesites on railroad's lands.

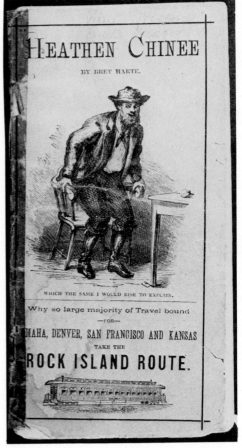

Although the United States railroads employed thousands of Chinese laborers in the construction of the western routes, they were held in low esteem. This is a copy of a Bret Harte story, published by the Chicago, Rock Island and Pacific, which denigrated the Chinese.

It is interesting to note that almost one hundred years ago land-sales schemes were directed to those who would settle and work the land whereas today the sales pitch is oriented toward leisure and retirement aspects. This may be a commentary on a change in our national values.

Nowadays collectors search for all advertising material offering inducements to new citizens and would-be citizens to settle on land bordering the railways. Through a study of these timetables, guides, tickets, and other ephemera we learn how the West was really won.

II

Railroad Labor-Union Memorabilia

Union and railroad-brotherhood collectibles are a specialty that falls within the larger category of railroad collectibles. This category might include badges, awards, pins, buttons, posters, handbills, and other reminders of the railroad workers' struggle for better working conditions and fair treatment from the management of a business that became the nation's largest industry in the period after the Civil War.

The organization of railroad workers took place in the decade following the Civil War, and many labor unions came into existence within a short space of time. The Brotherhood of the Footboard, which later became the Brotherhood of Locomotive Engineers, was the first of the railroad unions to be formed; it was organized in Detroit in 1863. This was followed by the Brotherhood of Locomotive Firemen in 1869. During the next ten years these organizations grew until they were strong enough to combat some of the inequities perpetrated by railroad management.

An economic slump in 1877 was given as an excuse by railroad management to cut the workers' pay by 10 percent on two different

Three buttons worn by members of three different railroad unions.

occasions. Soon afterward, management attempted to cut its expenses even more by running trains that were twice the normal length and using only one crew. Workers on the Baltimore and Ohio were the first to walk off their jobs, and a strike on the Pennsylvania soon followed. As the strike spread, and vital railroad traffic came to a halt in many parts of the East, the governor of Maryland called out the National Guard to protect the property of the railroads. The inevitable mob formed; stones were used by them as weapons; and the guards countered this attack with guns. Ten workers were killed.

A similar riot took place in Pittsburgh, and many railroad workers and guardsmen were killed. Violence then spread to St. Louis and Chicago, and President Hayes called out the army, so that troops could protect the strikebreakers. The strike collapsed, but from then on, it became customary for railroad management to call on the militia for help in any serious labor difficulties. Many of the armories that were built thereafter in major cities across the country were meant to house soldiers, who would then be ready for the task of protecting railroad property whenever a strike occurred.

The 1877 riots led to the formation of even stronger railroad unions, and the Knights of Labor grew in a single year from one hundred thousand to seven times that number. Throughout the

TO THE
TRAVELING
PUBLIC !

We, the Engineers of the North-West, appeal to the judgment of the traveling portion of the community, concerning the recent action of Officers of the

M. S. & N. I. RAILROAD.

The services required of the Engineers of the said Road have been DOUBLED. This new system obliges them to be on duty from thirty-six to forty hours, without rest or sleep. This you must allow is beyond human endurance.

Are you willing to trust your lives to the care of men so overburdened with labor, so taxed beyond their physical ability ?

To supply the places of the old and tried Engineers who would not submit to this new REGIME, the Company has hired BRAKEMEN, TRAINMASTERS, CHECK-CLERKS, or any thing that had any remote idea of running an engine.

To the competency of these extempore runners, the disabled, burnt, broken-down, and, but for God's providence, exploded engines, that are now strewn along their line of Railroad, bear palpable witness.

Poster printed on behalf of striking engineers on the Michigan, Southern and Northern Indiana Railroad protesting rule requiring men to work up to forty hours without rest.

remainder of the century the railroad brotherhoods continued to grow, and they became extremely effective in gaining advantages for their members. The unions were social as well as practical organizations, and today there are many tangible reminders of the closely knit fraternities that represented all classifications of occupations of the men who built the railroads and worked on the trains.

Perhaps the largest category of railroad brotherhood collectibles is the service button given to members for long periods of membership. Badges worn in parades and at conventions are also available. Posters and handbills announcing meetings and conventions are preserved by today's collectors, but all railway fraternal memorabilia is in demand since it represents an important period in American labor history.

Lapel buttons issued to members of the Brotherhood of Railroad Trainmen as evidence of up to thirty years of membership in the union.

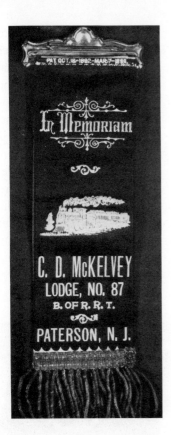

The Brotherhood of Railroad Trainmen was one of this country's earliest and strongest labor unions. This is a group of badges worn by union delegates to conventions and Labor Day observances.

12

Depot and Train Signs

T HE RAILROAD depot was the hub of small-town social life in the heyday of railroading. The station agent was in charge of this small world and the title of "agent" only referred to one who ran a depot in a small or medium-sized town. When a particularly able agent was transferred to a large station in a city he was promoted to superintendent.

Agents had a great many duties to perform. They were ticket sellers, bookkeepers, and switch-tenders. In addition, an agent was the telegraph operator, baggage master, agent for the express service and postal service, and he was also expected to tend to the grounds outside the station.

Judging from the amount of posters and signs that can still be found, the agent of a small railroad station was also responsible for tacking up and removing the many messages the railroads wished to communicate to their passengers. Outside firms also added their advertising posters to those printed by the railroads. As dissatisfaction with management began to lead to meetings of railroad employees, notices of brotherhood and union meetings, as well as posters expressing general and specific grievances, were tacked on the depot walls as well.

All depot and train posters and signs are in great demand today by collectors. Many represent the regional and national prejudices of what is hopefully a bygone era. Signs such as "COLORED" or "This Part of the Car for WHITE PEOPLE" illustrate the conformity of the railroad management with the prejudices prevalent at the time. Railroads protected the fair sex by establishing separate waiting rooms for women in the larger depots and stations. In the days when it was considered daring and risky for a woman to travel alone, this type of segregation was undoubtedly appreciated.

Many of the train signs printed and posted by management were in the cause of self-preservation and illustrate the habits of some of their uncouth passengers. "NOTICE! Please do not Spit on the Floor or Stove" or "NOTICE. Passengers are requested not to Vomit in the Urinals, but to use Water Closets" are certainly self-explanatory. Other depot and train posters offer rewards for vandals who preyed on the property of the railroads. Naturally, there were many "Wanted" posters for train robbers, and those that advertise for the apprehension of men who have since become well-known folk heroes are in special demand by today's collectors.

Special excursion rates were announced on posters that were prominently displayed in depots. All changes were announced in bold black lettering. An Erie Railway poster announces that effective March 25, 1868, various fares would be reduced because of "river competition." The notice begins on a rather gleeful note, "HA! HA! HA! Good news for Travelers!"

Through its printed posters the railway system could communicate with its passengers about rate changes, timetable changes, and special trains. Express companies could advise of seasonal services that were available in various regions. An especially interesting "sign of the times" is an 1884 poster meant to be read by fruit shippers who used the New York, West Shore, and Buffalo Railway Company. The poster announced the time schedule and special rates offered to accommodate growers in the Hudson River Valley who wanted to ship their produce to the Boston market. The rate was "60 cents per 100 Lbs. EMPTIES RETURNED FREE."

All posters having to do with the early days of railroading are in demand today. Few of these paper placards have survived, although hundreds of thousands were printed. Permanent depot and train signs made of wood or metal also have high priority on collectors' lists. Many of these have been salvaged from stations that have long since been torn down, and they are nostalgic reminders of the time when the railroad was the key to this country's development.

Many of the more durable steel-enameled and wood express-company and depot signs have survived and make attractive and historical wall decorations for rail fans.

BAGGAGE ROOM.

AGENT NO.
1137
NOW ON DUTY

SLEEPING CARS
FOR
PHILADELPHIA
WASHINGTON & MIAMI

Nineteenth-century railroads often used a combination of trains and steamers to get passengers to their destinations. This poster shows passenger cars being ferried on the transfer steamer "Maryland."

The Chicago and Alton was the first railroad to employ Pullman sleeping cars. This nineteenth-century poster places emphasis on this service.

THIS PART OF THE CAR
FOR
WHITE PEOPLE

COLORED

Some old depot and train signs are a sad reminder of the days of the "Jim Crow" rules on the railroads.

NOTICE.

Passengers are requested not to Vomit in the Urinals, but to use Water Closets.

Some passenger notices were concerned with maintaining a basic level of sanitation.

NOTICE!

Please do not Spit on the Floor or Stove

218

NOTICE

The Freight Train from Rome due at Watertown at **1:53 P. M.**, will be run on time on Thursday, the **30th** inst., accidents excepted ; and a sufficient number of **COACHES** to accommodate those wishing to attend the

MASS MEETING

will be attached.

ADDISON DAY, Supt. R.W. & O.R.R.

Watertown, Oct. 28, 1862,

The possibility of accidents occurring on a railroad in 1862 was treated very matter-of-factly in this poster issued by the Rome, Watertown and Ogdensburg Railroad.

This 1872 handbill indicates that vandalism of railroad property is not a recent problem.

$25.00 REWARD!

Will be paid for the apprehension and conviction of the person, or persons, who broke the Glass in certain Passenger Cars and in the Car House of the Boston & Albany Railroad Co. at South Framingham, between Saturday, April 27th, and Monday, April 29th, 1872.

A. FIRTH, Ass't Sup't.

Boston, May 3, 1872.

REWARD FOR ARREST
OF THE
TRAIN ROBBERS
TAKE NOTICE.

Early on the morning of Tuesday, September 12th, 1893, train No. 14, of the LAKE SHORE & MICHIGAN SOUTHERN RAILWAY CO. was stopped and its engineer was shot and the UNITED STATES EXPRESS CO. was robbed of about TEN THOUSAND DOLLARS, at Kessler's Siding, between Brimfield and Kendallville, in Indiana.

The undersigned will pay jointly a reward of ONE THOUSAND DOLLARS for each arrest and conviction of any of the guilty parties engaged in said robbery.

Address W. H. Canniff, Gen'l Supt. Lake Shore & Michigan Southern Railway Co., Cleveland, O.; E. W. Mitchell, Gen'l Supt. United States Express Co., Cleveland, O., or C. H. Crosby, Vice-President and Gen'l Mgr., United States Express Co., Chicago.

LAKE SHORE & MICHIGAN SOUTHERN RAILWAY COMPANY.
UNITED STATES EXPRESS COMPANY.

FURTHER REWARD.

In addition to the reward above provided for, the UNITED STATES EXPRESS COMPANY will pay for the return of any part of the money above mentioned as stolen, a further reward which shall equal ten per cent of the moneys which may be so returned. **THE UNITED STATES EXPRESS COMPANY.**

Geo. K. Cole & Co., Stationers and Printers,
56 & 58 Dearborn St., Chicago.

Reward poster recounting a violent robbery of a Lake Shore and Michigan Southern Railway train in 1893.

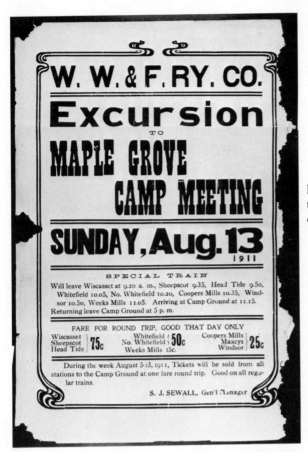

Excursion handbill of 1911 has typical Art Nouveau border design.

Handbill for Nevada railroad offers a 50¢ fare on a Fourth of July excursion in 1887.

Holiday excursions were promoted vigorously by the railroads. This 1889 Central Vermon Railroad handbill offers a $12.00 round-trip fare from Boston to Montreal for a winter carnival.

HA! HA! HA!

GOOD NEWS FOR TRAVELERS!

FARE REDUCED

VIA

ERIE

RAILWAY.

River competition having been again resumed and rates of fare reduced, the Managers of the Erie Railway have decided to promptly meet every attempt of this character to divert business, and therefore will, until further notice, issue SPECIAL TICKETS at the following Reduced Rates:

DUNKIRK TO NEW YORK,	- -	**$8.00**
BUFFALO do	- -	**7.00**
SALAMANCA do	- -	**7.00**
ATTICA do	- -	**6.25**
BATAVIA do	- -	**6.25**
ROCHESTER do	- -	**6.00**
LEROY do	- -	**6.00**
CALEDONIA do	- -	**5.75**

These Tickets will be VALID FOR A CONTINUOUS PASSAGE TO DESTINATION, by any Train on the day of their issue.

FOUR EXPRESS TRAINS DAILY

Through to New York without change of Coaches.

Through Tickets can be obtained at the Company's Offices, 143 Main Street, 65 Exchange Street, and Depot Corner Exchange and Michigan Streets, Buffalo, also at the Company's Offices in Dunkirk, Salamanca, Niagara Falls, Attica, Batavia, Leroy, Caledonia, and Rochester.

H. RIDDLE,   **A. J. DAY,**   **WM. R. BARR,**
Gen'l Sup't   Western Pass. Ag't, Chicago   Gen'l Passenger Agent
New York, March 25th, 1868

Erie Railway poster of March 1868 announces fare reduction due to competition from the steamers which resumed their service after the ice had left the rivers.

223

Intense competition in the nineteenth century caused the railroads to offer special inducements to shippers. Fruit growers in New York State could ship produce to Boston at a low rate and have their empty cartons returned to them free.

—:— TO —:—

FRUIT SHIPPERS.

COMMENCING

September 1st, 1884

—— THE ——

NEW YORK, WEST SHORE & BUFFALO

RAILWAY COMPANY

Will put on a SPECIAL TRAIN for Fruit Shipments

TO

BOSTON!

Train will leave as follows:

Newburgh,..	12.15 P. M.	Kingston, ...	1.55 P. M.
Marlborough, ...	12.40 "	Catskill,...........	3.00 "
Milton, ...	12.50 "	West Athens,.....	3.27 "
Highland,.........	1 05 "	Coxsackie,........	3.45 "
West Park,......	1 23 "	New Baltimore, ...	4.00 "
Esopus,......	1 30 "	Coeymans........	4.10 "
Ulster Park,......	1.36 "		

And will ARRIVE AT BOSTON at about 6 A.M. in time for the early morning market.

Rate from above named stations to Boston

60 Cents per 100 Lbs.

EMPTIES RETURNED FREE.

Shippers, by this arrangement, will secure express train service at ordinary freight rates.

B. H. BAIL,
Ass't Gen'l Freight Agent.

P. E. SCHOONMAKER,
Division Freight Agent.

Kingston Freeman Print, Rondout.

THREE KINDS OF FOOLS!

1. Fools
2. Damned Fools
3. SOLDIERS WHO RIDE on TOPS and SIDES of CARS

A Great Many American Soldiers Have Already Been Killed as a Result of Riding On Top of Cars.

There is Only Six Inches Clearance Between Tops and Sides of Cars, and Tunnel Arches.

There is Only Six Inches Clearance Between Tops and Sides of Cars and Bridge Superstructures.

There is Only a Slight Clearance Between Sides of Cars and Signal Towers.

IF YOU EXPECT TO SEE THE NEXT BLOCK, KEEP YOURS INSIDE

Signs from World War I troop train urging soldiers to keep their heads and hands inside the train.

HUNS are WAITING

TRENCHES AHEAD

SPEED UP

You won't if you ride on top of or stick your head out of cars

KEEP YOUR IVORY IN

Only Six Inches Clearance Between Tops and Sides Cars and Tunnel Arches and Bridges and Signal Towers

13

Railroad-Mail Collectibles

IT WAS not long after the American railroad industry began its great growth that plans for using the system to transport the mail were put forward. Until 1836 all the United States Post Office Department's mail was carried by horse-drawn vehicles, riders on horseback, or steamboats. To facilitate this method of mail delivery, the post office designated and maintained thousands of miles of highways that were known as post roads.

The annual report of the postmaster general in 1836 pointed out the proliferation of rail lines along the eastern seaboard and looked forward to the completion of the railroad between New York and Washington, which was then underway. The report emphasized the importance of the route for rapid mail service and predicted that the run between the two cities could probably be done in sixteen hours, instead of several days by stage or steamer.

The full feasibility of transporting the mail by rail was recognized by Congress in 1838, when it passed an act that declared every railroad as a post route. Indeed sometime before a railroad was fully operational, it automatically received a contract from the Post Office Department permitting it to carry mail.

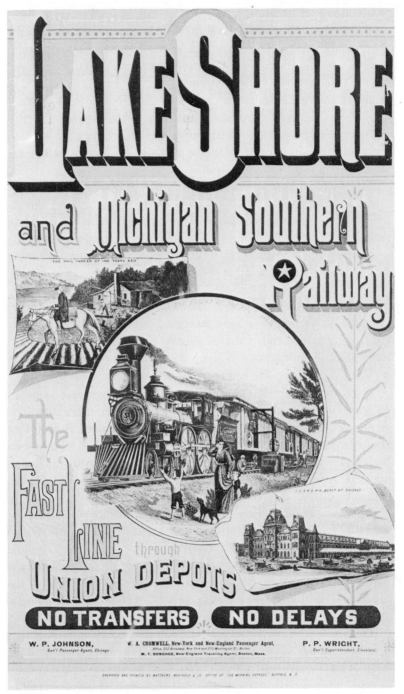

Lake Shore and Michigan Southern Railway poster features their slogan "The Flight of the Fast Mail." At the left is the mail carrier of 100 years ago on horseback traversing a wooden corduroy path. In the center the train is picking up a sack of mail while traveling at full speed. At the right is the Union Depot in Chicago.

It was not until 1862 that the plan of using specially built railway cars as traveling post offices to sort mail en route was adopted in this country; the method was in use in England and Canada considerably earlier. The first American railway post office was put into service on the run between Quincy, Illinois, and St. Joseph, Missouri, on the tracks of the Hannibal and St. Joseph Rail Road. W. A. Davis, a clerk in the St. Joseph post office, is credited with the idea of sorting the mail destined for the overland stagecoaches en route. In that way a considerable amount of time was saved in St. Joseph, where the stages began their journeys west.

The greatest improvement in the railway mail system took place under the administration of Colonel George S. Bangs, of Illinois, who became general railway mail superintendent in 1871. Bangs worked hard to refine, improve, and upgrade the speed and security of the service; he instituted worker incentive and merit programs that were a forerunner of the civil service system.

In 1874 Bangs negotiated with Commodore Vanderbilt, president of the New York Central, the Hudson River, and the Lake Shore railroads, to arrange for a fast mail train to travel from New York to Chicago over the rails of those lines. The Commodore was not enthusiastic but his son, William H. Vanderbilt, who was vice-president, supported the plan and put it into operation.

To do this, the railroad constructed twenty special mail cars at its own expense and scheduled a special train to leave New York City at four in the morning and arrive in Chicago about twenty-four hours later. Vanderbilt ran the train punctually for ten months, during which time the Pennsylvania Railroad established its own fast mail train, and the pressure from other railroads diluted the Central's load and caused the operation to become unprofitable. The final blow was a reduction by Congress in the compensation to the railroads for the carrying of mail. This situation only lasted until 1877, when Congress voted additional funds so that the mail might travel more expeditiously on the main trunk lines. By 1888 the railway mail service employed over five thousand clerks and distributed the mail along more than 126,000 miles of railroad trackage.

The life of a railway postal clerk back in the nineteenth century was far from easy. Traveling in an unheated car directly behind the engine and tender, they were often among the casualties of the frequent derailments and collisions. There was no government compensation for death or disability, no pensions, and their pay started at $900 a year and only went up to $1300 when they became crew supervisors. Crews were required to make three round trips on their division (as, for example, between New York and Syracuse) before they were given six days off. During their time on duty when not actually traveling, they slept in dormitories located in the post office buildings and were always on call to work extra shifts whether off duty or not.

In spite of the hardships, hazardous conditions, and low pay, most of the railway postal clerks were credited as a group with being bright, industrious, and loyal. The only drawback to the operation in terms of personnel was the political spoils system. Civil service reforms were yet to be introduced into government hiring practices, and each time there was a change of party in the national elections, many clerks lost their jobs to political friends of the new administration.

This colorful and significant function of the railroads in the carrying of the United States mail is just about extinct. Just as the railroads superseded the stagecoach and the steamboat, the airlines and the trucking industry have taken over the hauling of mail for the Post Office Department. Airplanes can cover great distances far faster, and trucks can take the mail directly from one post-office loading dock to another without additional handling at railroad depots.

Recapturing the era of fast mail trains can be accomplished by forming a collection of memorabilia associated with that endeavor. Among the items sought by collectors are hardware from railway post offices, such as the mail sacks and the hooks mounted on the cars to snatch the sacks from the depots as the cars sped by. Especially desirable would be the interior fittings of a post office car. These would include the bank of pigeon holes into which the sorted mail was placed.

If parts of the old railway post offices can not be found, collectors can sometimes be satisfied by accumulating contemporary photographs or engravings of the interior and exterior views of the mail cars. The photograph, shown in this chapter, of the interior of one of these cars was taken in 1906 before it was delivered to the railroads by its manufacturer, the Pullman Company. This historically

The Post Office Department also used mail cars on some trolley lines: This is a
photo of a railway post office on the Brooklyn, N. Y., Rapid Transit System.

This postcard was canceled on a street-car railway post office in Pittsburgh, Pa., in
1913.

The railway post office car on the opposite page was built by the Pullman
Company in 1906 and was still equipped with gas lighting fixtures. This photo is
from the old Pullman glass negative.

important photograph was printed from a collection of over three thousand 8″ by 10″ glass negatives that were once the property of the Pullman Company. Fortunately these invaluable plates were salvaged before their intended destruction and are now owned by a leading dealer in railroadiana.

Of interest to both philatelists and railroadiana collectors are the envelopes and other pieces of mail bearing railroad cancellations. Since the postmark included the name of the railroad on which the

Four pieces of mail bearing cancellations by railway post offices in Texas, Vermont, Colorado, and North Carolina.

letter was carried and the date it was cancelled, each item can be accurately attributed as to time and origin. Also, for the specialist in railroad philately there are first and last day covers that represent the story of the railroad's postal history, and many stamps honoring various historical aspects of railroading history. Included within this category of collecting are the envelopes issued by the railroads for their own use and the use of travelers.

233

Railway Post Office commemorative items are of interest to railroadiana collectors and philatelists. In addition to anniversary and first day issues there are the sadder last day covers.

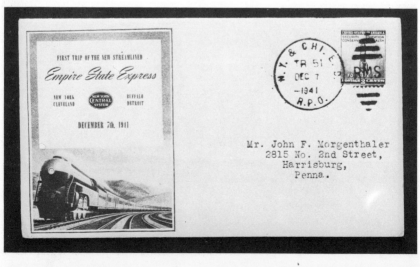

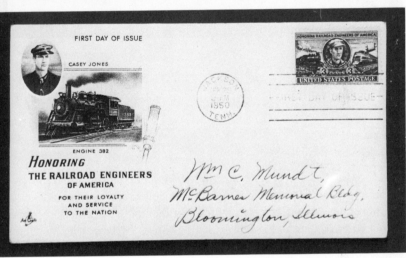

14

Toy and Model Trains

T HERE is a category of railroadiana collectibles that transcends pure railroad memorabilia and attracts collectors who would not be interested in switch keys, lanterns, timetables, or other important railroad artifacts. This aspect of the hobby attracts some collectors who could not care less when the Twentieth Century Limited was discontinued or the New York, Ontario and Western Railway Company folded up. These collectors are the ones who are sometimes thought of as "small boys grown up" and who collect old toy trains.

These are not the model railroaders who devote themselves to constructing fantastically detailed working layouts on which their tiny trains can be operated. Instead these collectors spend their time, energy, ingenuity, and money tracking down vintage models of Lionel, Ives, American Flyer, and other more esoteric makes of toy trains.

While some purists will collect electrified models, others will also collect windups and even pull toys if they represent old trains or trolley cars. The point is that they must have originally been made as toys and be old or rare enough to qualify as a genuine collectible.

Top, Turn-of-the-century open-side pull-toy trolley made by the Morton E. Converse Co., of Winchendon, Mass. *Bottom,* pull-toy trolley made in the 1920's.

With the widespread interest in this hobby, not only dealers in railroadiana but dealers in general antiques have been drawn into the business of trying to maintain a representative inventory. The demand is apparently so great that dealers are trying to attract the owners of such pieces into offering them for sale by advertising outside the usual railroadiana and antiques journals. Ads have been appearing in the "Wanted to Buy" section of local newspapers, seeking to purchase those long-forgotten toys that may still be stored in basements, closets, and attics.

Since few of the old electric trains can now be found in complete sets or in working order and were never very accurate reproductions anyway, they must be collected mostly for their nostalgic value and as an attempt to recapture a happy childhood. In a way the interest in them might be compared to the recollection of "Rosebud" by the hero in the motion picture *Citizen Kane*.

The challenge for some collectors, of course, is to repair and put back into working condition an old electric locomotive that hasn't run in fifty years. For most, however, there is enough satisfaction in merely acquiring an additional piece, cleaning it up, and putting it on the shelf with the rest of the collection. Too much restoration diminishes a toy train's value in the market, and the experienced dealer or collector will recoil from a repainted piece and say, "Why did they have to do that to a 1925 Ives passenger car?"

Among the types of collectible toy trains that predate the electric-powered models are the simple trackless pull toys that made their appearance not long after real trains were introduced around 1825. These tin locomotives and trolley cars were popular through the latter half of the nineteenth century, until the powered variety began to add realism to their operation and made inroads on their sales.

The earliest self-propelled toy trains were of the clockwork or windup variety and were introduced in the United States in 1856. They were made, appropriately, by a Connecticut clock manufacturer and were not designed to run on rails. In 1868 the Ives firm was founded in Plymouth, Connecticut, which was also a clockmaking center, and in 1870 the firm moved to Bridgeport, Connecticut. There it remained in business until 1932, and during this span of sixty-four years became a leader and innovator in the toy train industry.

Clockwork-driven locomotive made in Bristol, Conn., by George W. Brown & Co., c. 1865.

Ives produced clockwork trains continuously until its demise, and these windups, which were adapted to run on tracks in 1901, are today all collectors' items. This is true, also, of other Ives nonelectric trains, such as cast-iron pull toys and trains driven by real steam power.

From about 1870 through the 1920's steam-powered toys were quite popular. They were sold in great numbers and advertised in Sears, Roebuck and other mail-order catalogs. At the present time, when there is considerable awareness of the safety aspect of toys, it is difficult to understand how parents would allow their children to play with these steam engines. Their operation involved heating a small boiler containing water with an alcohol-fueled flame. In the hands of youngsters, the possibility of serious burns and fires is frightening to contemplate. Nevertheless, several firms were active in this area of manufacture, and examples of steam-powered trains made by Weeden, Beggs, Garlick, and the Steam-Electric Company are all eagerly sought.

Toy trains, powered by electricity, were first made in the United States as early as the middle of the nineteenth century, but it was not until 1896 that they were produced in any substantial quantity. At that time the Carlisle and Fitch Company of Cincinnati, Ohio, began manufacturing electric trolley cars and later expanded their line to include steam-type locomotive and other varieties of trolleys and trains.

The Lionel Company, which eventually came to dominate the toy electric-train business, was started in 1901 by Joshua Lionel Cowen. For the first few years Lionel made electric-powered gondola cars, trolley cars, derrick cars, and a Baltimore and Ohio locomotive. All this early production was designed to run on a track 2⅞ inches wide. This width was abandoned in 1906 when Lionel brought out a line of trains and trolleys designed for a 2⅛-inches-wide three-rail track which came to be known as standard gauge. All track widths are measured from the inner edge of the outside rails.

Other manufacturers who entered the electric-train business between 1905 and the beginning of World War I were Howard, Knapp, Voltamp, American Flyer, and Ives. Of these, only American Flyer and Ives continued in the business for any substantial length of time. American Flyer started in Chicago in 1907 making clockwork trains and in 1918 introduced a line of electric trains. The firm was bought by the A. C. Gilbert Company of Erector Set fame in 1938 and moved to the Gilbert factories in New Haven, Connecticut. Gilbert continued marketing the American Flyer line until 1965 when they went out of the toy-train business.

In the years between 1924 and 1936 there was one other important electric-train manufacturer. This was the Dorfan Company of Newark, New Jersey, which was formed by two brothers who had earlier been employed by a German toy manufacturer. The Dorfan line of toy electric trains was distinguished by their use of die-cast engine bodies, rather than the light tinplate favored by other makers. Their emphasis on quality motors and other engineering refinements made their engines the most powerful of any then being manufactured. Passenger cars, also, were of very substantial construction and highly detailed in terms of decorative trim. Since Dorfan trains were only produced for about ten years, they are among the rarer and more desirable of collectible toy trains.

Many collectors consider the standard-gauge Lionel model 32 to be a classic among electric locomotives. Built in the mid-1920's, each of its two sets of four wheels was driven by a separate motor.

The Ives Company began manufacturing electric trains in 1910, and their earliest models were made to fit O-gauge track, which is 1⅜ inches wide. They are principally appreciated, however, for their line of big standard-gauge trains, which were first produced in 1921 and continued to be made until 1932. In 1928 Ives declared bankruptcy and was taken over by American Flyer, Hafner, and Lionel. The company was allowed to operate on its own until 1932, when Lionel assumed complete control and abandoned the use of the Ives name the following year.

In the time it actively produced electric toy trains no other company had more influence on the development and marketing of these products than Ives. Ives trains were noted for exceptional realism, engineering innovations, and an extremely liberal repair and replacement policy. Especially prized, also, are the high quality of lithography employed in the exterior decoration of Ives passenger and freight cars. Among collectors of Ives trains there are some who specialize in collecting as many different examples of freight cars and road names as they can find. With variations in types of cars, colors and heralds (railroad insignia), the number is almost limitless. The motto of the toy train company was "Ives Toys make Happy Boys."

Ives model 3241 standard-gauge electric locomotive was one of a series that helped establish Ives quality reputation in the decade between 1920 and 1930.

Left, Ives O-gauge eight-wheel passenger car. *Right,* German-made four-wheel observation car was part of clockwork train.

Left, Lionel standard-gauge Pullman car. *Right,* Ives standard-gauge observation car.

Lionel model 9E standard-gauge locomotive. Made during late-1920's and into the 1930's.

Standard-gauge Lionel baggage and observation cars. Both display a very high level in detail and finish.

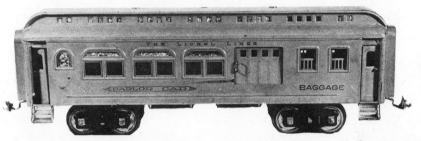

Lionel standard model 419 baggage and parlor car, made between 1925 and 1935.

To return to the Lionel make of electric trains, this company, under various managements, has been producing enormous quantities of trains and accessories for seventy-five years. Its output includes almost all popular gauges from the small, accurately scaled HO 16.5 mm. width to the huge standard-gauge trains. Every possible accessory such as tunnels, bridges, signals, stations, and switches has been represented in their line at one time or another. As the technology of railroading evolved from steam- to electric-powered locomotives and then to diesels, the Lionel line has reflected these changes. It is sometimes difficult to appreciate that a complete set of Lionel O-gauge trains which sold for perhaps $50 only twenty years ago is now worth five or six times that amount to collectors. Naturally, older and rarer sets and some individual pieces are worth considerably more.

Among the toy-train collectibles, such as locomotives, freight and passenger cars, and accessories, there is another item that is eminently desirable. This is the manufacturer's catalog. The more successful makers such as Ives, Lionel, and American Flyer realized quite early the sales appeal their catalogs held for potential buyers. Great effort was made to produce annual catalogs that were as exciting and enticing as possible. Catalogs in full color became

Four Lionel standard-gauge freight cars, including tank car, operating dump car, cattle car, and caboose.

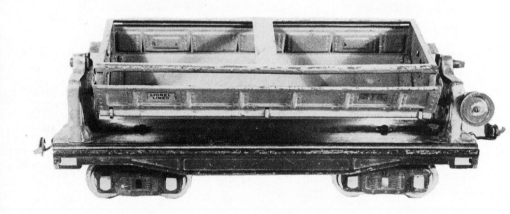

common, and this helped enhance the sales message. Boys would spend hours going through them, trying to decide which outfit they wanted most or assembling imaginary layouts.

Once given away free by the hundreds of thousands, or sold for only a few cents when ordered from the manufacturer by mail, some of these catalogs are now selling for more than a hundred dollars. Even reproductions or reprints of scarce issues are quoted at six dollars apiece in black and white. These old catalogs have value for the collector not just for nostalgia but as a definitive method for identifying and dating a particular manufacturer's equipment. They are also helpful in determining if an item is a production variation and thus rare, or was part of a regularly manufactured line.

Not only American-made vintage toy trains but also trains imported into the United States in large quantities prior to World War II are prized by collectors. The German manufacturers were the most active in this area, and among the most important lines today are Maerklin, Bing, and Carette. Other collectible foreign makers are Bassett-Lowke, Ltd., and Hornby of England, Seki of Japan, and Kraus, Trix and Fleischman Brothers of Germany.

The preceding discussion of toy trains centers on the type that collectors refer to as "tinplate." This category encompasses all pull

Ives and Lionel made hundreds of different toy-train accessories. This station, c. 1925, was probably made by Ives.

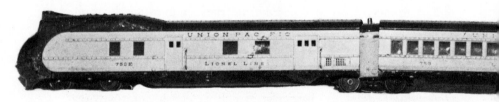

Famous Lionel O-gauge model of one of the first streamlined and completely articulated passenger trains, the Union Pacific's "City of Portland," produced from 1934 to 1941.

A group of trackside Lionel accessories, including crossing signs, lighted signal lamps, and operating semaphore.

Lionel O-gauge steam-type locomotive made about 1936.

This Lionel O-gauge "Hudson" type die-cast locomotive and tender was made during the 1940's. It is now among the more desirable items produced during this period.

Cover of 1927 Ives train catalog. Ives trains were made for sixty-four years—from 1868 to 1932.

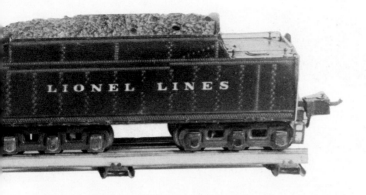

toys, key-wound clockwork, steam- or electric-powered varieties, and the track and accessories made to go with them. The term tinplate applies to an area of collecting in which working condition and absolute fidelity to scale is secondary to rarity, historical value, and condition. Tinplate collectors are not concerned with operating their trains; this function they leave to the model-railroad enthusiasts. Model railroaders, for the most part, work with considerably smaller units in the HO, HOn3, On3, N, and Z gauges. Some model railroaders maintain layouts in the larger O gauge, which is generally more expensive as a hobby than working with the more popular miniature sizes. O gauge is made on a scale of 1:48; HO is 1:87; N is 1:160; and Z is 1:220. Thus it can be seen how the size of miniature model trains has diminished in comparison with the toy tinplate trains.

There is a fairly recent development in the collection of model trains that is a departure from the emphasis on age and rarity associated with the old tinplate trains. This new mania is the collecting of brass model trains, most of which have been manufactured in Japan and other Far Eastern countries, such as Korea, and exported to eager collectors all over the world.

Shortly after the end of World War II, a large portion of Japanese industry was still in the process of trying to rebuild from the damage it suffered from American air raids. At that time a few Japanese manufacturers were looking for products which they could make from scrap or low-priority materials and which did not require

Cover and page 7 of 1929 Lionel catalog showing line-up of O-gauge electric locomotives.

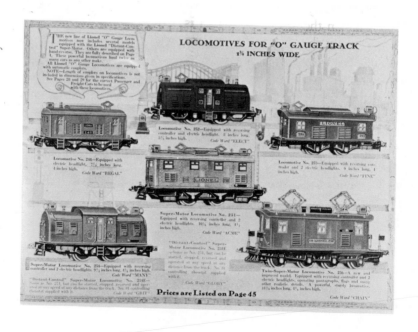

Cover and page 31 of 1950 Lionel catalog. None of the diesel locomotives shown sold for more than $47.50. Current prices are about six times more.

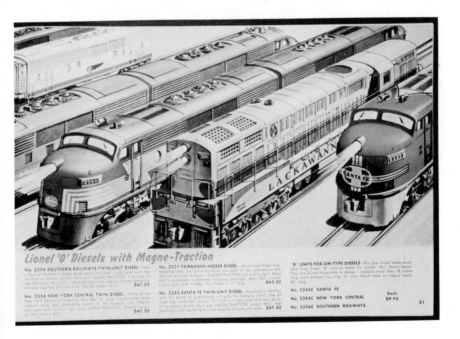

elaborate manufacturing facilities. With the encouragement of American servicemen stationed in Japan, a few workers began to produce miniature models of railroad locomotives, passenger and freight cars.

Fairly crude at first, these models evolved, in the shops of the more skilled and painstaking workmen, into enormously detailed and meticulously scaled model trains. Using the lost-wax method of casting in brass the outer shells of the cars, the utmost precision and fidelity to the mold was achieved. Working parts, such as the wheels and driving mechanism, lamps, tubing, and other trim were also faithfully rendered.

It was not long before model-railroad enthusiasts recognized their quality, and at the low prices then being asked, quickly bought all they could. At the same time the more enterprising distributors of model equipment went to Japan and contracted for as much of the output of the various manufacturers as they could procure. These distributors, who soon found themselves in the import business, began to suggest to their suppliers which models to make according to the mystique or classic qualities of particular locomotives and other equipment.

The brass-model collectors presently number in the thousands, and their particular enthusiasm differs from tinplate collectors or model-railroad operators. Dedicated brass-model collectors never run their trains and rarely handle or show them. Their objective is to preserve the models they own in as pristine, or mint, condition as possible. Value is enhanced if the trains still repose, unwrapped, in their original packing.

So valuable have some of the rarer issues become that they are traded and sold very much like gilt-edge securities or the limited editions of commemorative coins issued by private mints. Dealers and collectors run ads in the railroad-hobby magazines offering in arcane terms a PFM HO Crown GN S-1 4-8-4 for $340. This is a brass steam-type locomotive with PFM referring to Pacific Fast Mail, the importer. HO is the gauge; Crown, the manufacturer; GN stands for Great Northern Railway; and S-1 4-8-4, the model and wheel configuration of the steam engine.

Other major importers and makers whose brass models are commonly collected are Custom Brass, Gem, NPP (Nickel Plate

This is an O-gauge "scratch-built" locomotive model that was constructed by a hobbyist who either made or bought the parts and assembled it himself.

HO-gauge brass model of Union Pacific 4-8-8-4 "Big Boy," one of the largest steam locomotives ever built. Manufactured in Japan and imported by Gem Models.

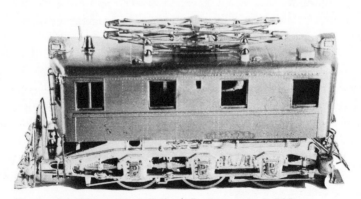

Brass model of Pennsylvania Railroad B-1 locomotive in HO gauge, imported by Alco.

253

Brass model in HO-gauge of a bus built by the Mack Truck Company and designed to operate on rails.

Products), NWSL (NorthWest Short Line), and Westside. All these brands and others are consistently advertised in listings that look very much like the stock quotations in the *Wall Street Journal*.

From this preoccupation with value, condition, and rarity, we can assume that a large percentage of the brass-model collectors are engaged in the pursuit not for the hobby aspect as much as for the promise of financial benefit. From an investment standpoint, those who started early have fared best. A collector will show a brass locomotive he bought for $75 eight or ten years ago that is now being offered by dealers for $250. Whether those presently buying at current levels will see their investment appreciate remains to be seen.

As the interest in brass models has evolved over the past few years, certain patterns of collecting have become apparent. Collectors are now attempting to upgrade their holdings by contracting for desirable specimens as soon as an importer announces that they are going to be available. This is usually several months before they actually arrive in dealers' shops. Selling out a complete production run of perhaps two thousand pieces on a subscription basis considerably ahead of the time it is actually delivered makes these pieces instant collectibles.

Factory-painted HO-gauge brass model of Great Northern 2-8-0 steam locomotive. Imported from Japan by Pacific Fast Mail.

Two brass models of the same engine, imported by Westside Model Co., showing relative difference between the larger O gauge and the smaller HO.

O-scale brass model of 2-6-6-T engine, used on the Denver, South Park and Pacific's narrow-gauge railroad in the 1880's, imported by LMB.

The desire to upgrade one's collection is caused principally by the fact that recent production is far superior in terms of detail and mechanical improvement to the earlier models. While the first production run of a particular model has some historical value and has appreciated due to rarity and dollar devaluation, the newer, more sophisticated models seem to be even more eagerly sought.

Another recent development by some manufacturers is to offer a model fully painted with the insignia and color trim of the railroad line that employed that type of equipment. This is an extra-cost option that the makers and importers have obviously found profitable and for which collectors are willing to pay. Previously all brass models were shipped unpainted in the plain brass finish and it was left to the owner to decide whether he himself would paint a purchase or leave it untouched.

About 80 percent of all brass models are made in HO gauge with the balance offered in the smaller HOn3, On3, or the larger O gauge. O gauge models, while more than twice as large and massive as HO, are relatively not that much more expensive. As an example, the highly desirable PFM Southern Pacific 4-8-8-4 "Big Boy" locomotive might be offered in a current rerun for $850 in HO gauge and $1000 in the O gauge. Many of today's collectors feel that a 50 percent bigger engine is well worth a 15 percent additional investment.

15

Conclusion

It should be obvious by now to the reader who might have been previously unfamiliar with railroad collectibles that there are literally thousands of items still available. Because of this great variety, it is almost necessary to specialize in one or two categories of railroadiana. Some collectors will concentrate on owning as many lanterns as possible, while others will search only for tickets, annual passes, or timetables. What all railroadiana collectors have in common, however, is a great love for trains and a nostalgia for the golden days of railroading. They also possess a determination to preserve through its artifacts the history of the railroads.

It is possible to divide all railroad collectibles into two very broad areas—hardware and paper memorabilia. The category of hardware includes such items as dining-car silver and china, lanterns, locks and keys, steam whistles, locomotive bells, and other parts of trains, railroad depots, and their furnishings. The ultimate collectible among hardware objects is the manufacturer's plate that may be all that is left of a locomotive that has been destroyed for scrap.

When financially hard-pressed, some railroads issued their own currency or scrip. The upper certificate is a $5 fare voucher good for one hundred miles of travel. The lower certificate is a $50 note.

Builder's plates are in short supply, and those few train buffs that do collect them usually include plates from locomotives built in all parts of the world.

There are thousands of items that fit into the category of paper memorabilia, and this is by far the more popular of the two major collectible areas. Further specialization is almost necessary if the collector is not to become inundated in old paper ephemera. Although all the major areas of this field of railroadiana have been discussed in previous chapters, collectors will continue to find unusual posters, handsome timetables, colorful calendars, and many other paper items, all adding something to the history of railroading. Within the past few years, name-train folders, printed by the railroads to promote the fast trains of this century, have been in demand.

In general, there are several art styles that are reflected in the thousands of paper items connected with the history of American railroads. Before the 1870's timetables were mostly printed in local newspapers, tickets were primitive receipts and were seldom standardized, and broadsides were posted in local depots or at some other central point in a town such as the general store. From the period beginning in 1880 and lasting until a few years after the turn of the century, the railroads emerged as the single most important industry in America. As the industry grew, so did its supply departments, and hundreds of different items were printed in the flowery and sinuous Art Nouveau style of the period. By the 1930's this style in the graphic arts had disappeared and the more streamlined Art Deco style of lettering became popular.

The early period of successful railroading coincided with the growth of the advertising industry, and after 1880 we have a huge supply of colorful lithographed posters, timetables, annual passes, tickets, and other railroad memorabilia. Most of these items are as decorative as they are historical. Turn-of-the-century paper objects connected with railroading are among the most sought-after of all train memorabilia.

There is another reason why timetables and other railroad paper items became less artistic after 1910. The railroads became more conservative in their spending, and the printed ephemera from that time on is a reflection of a "fewer frills" policy that most of the railroads adopted. During World War I only function was considered in the printing of railroad information, and the time-tables, especially, became smaller and less artistic.

The tendency to more elaborate printing was reestablished in the early 1920's when passenger service was at its height and competition caused many of the railroads to issue handsome folders and brochures. With the building of crack streamlined trains came advertising material in great quantities to promote the comfort and speed of the famous name trains. By this time the railroads were receiving strong competition from the automobile, and the begin-

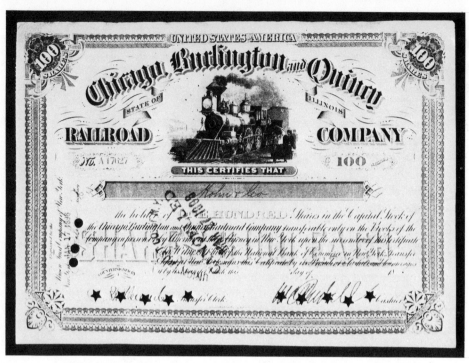

Though now only relics of failed companies, old stock certificates are collected for their decorative value and historical appeal. This group of certificates represents a minute fraction of the enormous capital invested in America's railroads in the nineteenth century. Although great fortunes were made, more were lost when most of these railroads failed. Now many collectors literally "paper their walls" with old railroad-stock certificates.

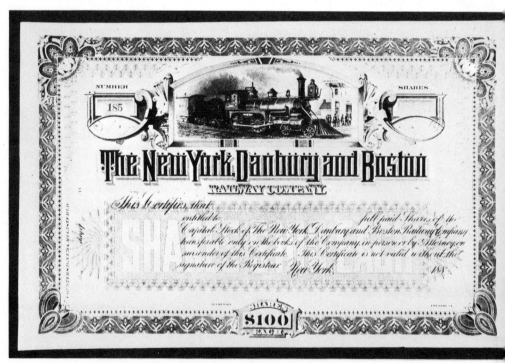

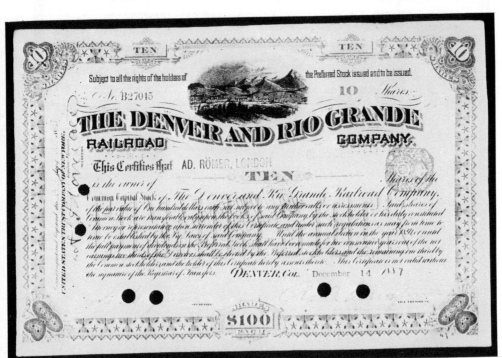

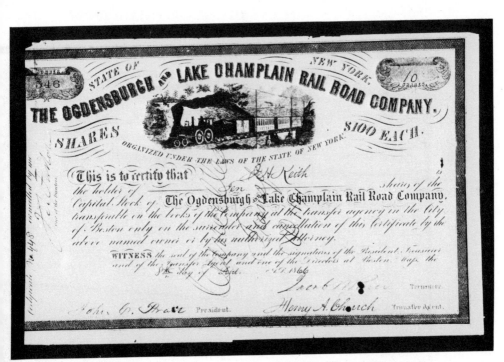

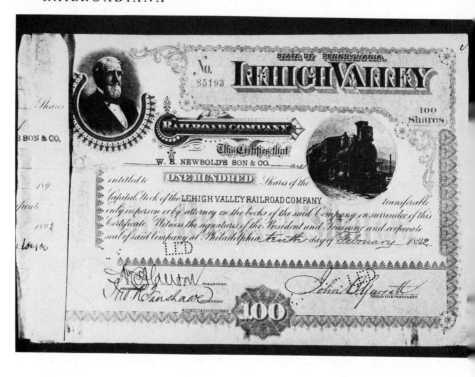

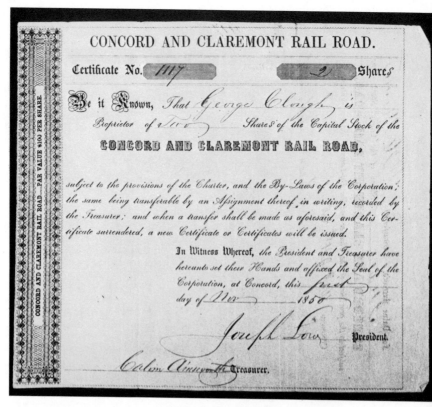

ning of the demise of passenger service finally took place with the advent of air travel following World War II.

By the early 1960's it was apparent that the railroad as a major form of travel was a part of our historic past, and collectors began to salvage what they could that would eventually tell the story of railroading history to younger generations. Having little sentiment for its own history, railroad management began to tear down old depots, and old locomotives and passenger cars were dismantled and scrapped. Dedicated collector historians kept whatever could be saved, and many of the earlier collections have already been incorporated into railroad museums.

Presently there are so many railroad museums and displays that a list of them would fill more than a single volume. The history of the railroads, especially the story of the age of steam, seems to have enormous appeal to a great many people. Certainly those Americans whose family history is somehow tied to the building and running of the railroads are among the most dedicated collectors we have today.

Most of the surviving railroads are today too involved with business problems to be interested in preserving their own history. They are prone to junk or sell objects that have no relevance to their day-to-day operations of running the trains. From time to time railroad companies have sold at auction many of the obsolete and useless objects that take up storage space, and these sales have become excellent sources for railroadiana collectors and dealers.

It is partly due to the efforts of railroad buffs that at least some of the depots recently slated for destruction have been saved and restored. Many such examples of regional architecture have already been destroyed by railroad lines beset with financial troubles, but at least some of the buildings have been purchased by interested citizens' groups or individuals. Some of the depots have been moved to other locations and converted to dwellings.

There is great interest today in preserving the artifacts of all outmoded methods of transportation. Those collectors involved in gathering and preserving the thousands of items associated with American railroading find it a fascinating and rewarding hobby. The history of railroading is reflective of America's social and business history, and each timetable, annual pass, switch lock and key, lantern, or dining-car menu adds to the general knowledge of the great part the railroads played in the growth of the nation.

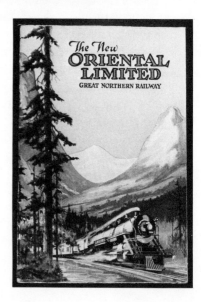

To relive the age of gracious travel on America's great passenger trains, many collectors seek the folders printed by the railroads to promote their famous "name" trains.

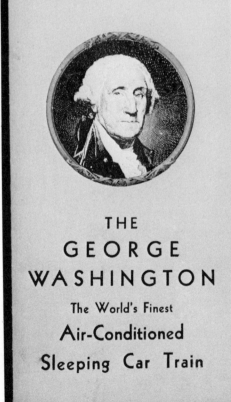

Index

(Page numbers in italics indicate illustrations; *_132_ indicates the illustration is in the color section, following page 132.)